MISSING BELIEVED LOST

MISSING BELIEVED LOST

THE GREAT BRITISH FILM SEARCH

Edited by

ALLEN EYLES

and

DAVID MEEKER

Foreword by

J. PAUL GETTY Jnr KBE

Introduction by

CLYDE JEAVONS

BFI PUBLISHING

First published
in 1992 by the
British Film Institute
21 Stephen Street
London W1P 1PL

Copyright ©
British Film Institute
1992

British Library
Cataloguing in
Publication Data

Eyles, Allen
Missing believed lost.
I. Title
011.37

ISBN 0-85170-306-2

Designed by
John Gibbs
Typeset by
Fakenham Photosetting
Printed and bound
in Great Britain by
The Trinity Press,
Worcester

Publication of this
book would not have
been possible without
J. Paul Getty Jnr KBE
and Wilf Stevenson,
whose assistance we
gratefully acknowledge.
All stills are taken from
the Stills, Posters and
Design Department of
the National Film Archive.

Cover picture: Eric Blore
in *A Gentleman's
Gentleman* (1939)

Frontispiece: Rene Ray
in *Born Lucky* (1932)

Contents

7   Foreword

9   Introduction

11   THE FILM-MAKERS

17   THE FILMS

99   APPENDICES

     The Documentaries

     The Television Programmes

105   Index

Foreword

As with everyone who really cares about British films, I am totally dedicated to the work of the National Film Archive, which is achieving so much in the way of preserving our British film heritage. This little book, drawing our attention to some of the key feature films that appear to be lost and gone forever, comes as something of a shock! Are we never going to see Alfred Hitchcock's *The Mountain Eagle*? How can twelve, yes, *twelve* of Michael Powell's quota quickies from the formative 1930s be missing? And the first feature films made by the young Bernard Vorhaus shortly after he first came to Britain in the late 1920s? And those priceless Walter Forde comedies? How frustrating that we can see only a few precious reels saved by the Archive of his long-lost classic version of *The Ghost Train* (1931), in which the delightful Jack Hulbert set a standard for playing farce. And how we'd like to see the cheeky Max Miller in *Educated Evans* and *Get Off My Foot*. And what has happened to most of the films made at Teddington Studios by the talented Roy William Neill, William Beaudine and Ralph Ince?

The traditions of popular British cinema – Alfred Hitchcock, Will Hay, Moore Marriott and Graham Moffatt, Tom Walls and Ralph Lynn, Jessie Matthews, Walter Forde, The Crazy Gang and so many others for which we have such deep affection – have helped to shape the nation's consciousness, whether we know it or not. The National Film Archive needs all the help and good fortune it can get in its endeavours to trace the untraceable – if just one of the missing films can be located and properly preserved, I shall be as thrilled as they.

J. Paul Getty

Introduction

THERE IS A semi-serious belief among film archivists that the moment you say 'lost film' – presto! – the title in question perversely comes to light on a laboratory shelf or pops up in a private collection. There is, of course, a modicum of truth in this – if you don't name the film, the possessor won't know it's 'lost' and being looked for; but if it were invariably the case, there would be no need for this book, which cites a hundred instances where the magic words haven't yet worked.

Another legend (this one beloved of journalists) says that there are dozens of lost and neglected classic films lying in dusty vaults or attics waiting to be rediscovered – a *Greed* here, a Griffith there, the Hitchcock That Never Was. Thankfully, this is also mythical, notwithstanding the occasional *Napoléon*: curators and film historians have already covered that particular ground thoroughly, and all the best-known films have, by their very nature, tended to survive, if not always as their creators intended.

What this book deals with in the main is what one international film archivist has called the 'orphans' of cinema: the bread-and-butter features which enjoyed a screen life and then faded from view, but which have an honourable place in the still-primeval history of the twentieth century's unique art form, the motion picture.

Between these pages are some of the lost orphans of British cinema, a careful selection by the National Film Archive's Keeper of Feature Films, David Meeker, of one hundred movies (plus some documentaries, and a smattering of lost and lamented television programmes) which have remained unseen for decades and which we would all dearly wish to see preserved, for the chance to appraise and enjoy them once again. A few of them are, as it happens, missing classics of the silent era, such as George Pearson's *Reveille* (1924) and *A Study in Scarlet* (1914), not to mention the one tantalisingly lost Hitchcock picture, *The Mountain Eagle* (1926), but most of them derive from the first twenty years of sound, the golden age of cinema-going when there was no such thing as an unpopular film.

They range from the twelve early apprentice films ('quota quickies' as they were called) of one of Britain's greatest film-makers, Michael Powell, which continue to elude the Archive; a clutch of Walter Forde comedies, including the reels still missing from the film everyone wants to find, *The Ghost Train* of 1931; Errol Flynn's first film appearance in Britain, *Murder at Monte Carlo* (1935); a pre-Pinkie Richard Attenborough performance in *The Hundred Pound Window* (1943); a precious Max Miller, *Educated Evans* (1936); three early features of the fast-shooting location genius, Bernard Vorhaus; Ralph Ince's *It's Not Cricket* (1937); Roy William Neill's *A Gentleman's Gentleman* (1939), with the British-born Hollywood favourite Eric Blore; *The Bells* (1931), co-directed by Oscar M. Werndorff, Hitchcock's art director on many films . . . and dozens more, all accurately researched and entertainingly described by film historian and critic Allen Eyles. To find just one of these intact would justify the cost of publishing *Missing Believed Lost*.

It is reasonable to ask why (and how) the films mentioned in this book, like many parallel films in other countries, have become lost, especially those which fall into the period of sixty years or so since the first preservation archives came into existence. There are several reasons, all equally depressing: the indifference, until recent years, of the film industry itself to the survival of its past product; the subsequent neglect, loss, decay or wilful destruction of countless films (it has been estimated that two-thirds of all silent cinema is irretrievably lost, perhaps a quarter of all sound films); the fact that all studio-made 35mm films until 1951 were produced on highly flammable, chemically unstable nitrate cellulose stock; and the fact that film archives themselves, born and raised in poverty and with no statutory rights to acquire prints, have been forced to operate rigorous selection policies: it is not without a trace of shame and regret that the NFA itself must admit to having rejected in the past some of the films listed between these covers. The tragedy is that this book is necessary at all.

Matters have improved a little in the 90s: there is still no system of legal deposit in the UK, but the industry has (thanks partly to the commercial re-release possibilities of television and video) seen the error of its ways, and relations with archives are good; the NFA can just about afford to preserve at least all the British films in its collection; and thanks to the International Federation of Film Archives (FIAF), the lost films of many countries are altruistically being hunted all over the world.

What hope, meanwhile, for the films in this book? One encouraging factor is that, even without it, eagerly sought-after films are occasionally turning up. The Archive has, in recent years, found some of the Powell quota quickies (*The Night of the Party*, *The Love Test*); Paul Stein's *The Lisbon Story*; Anatole Litvak's *Sleeping Car*, with Ivor Novello; two Walter Forde comedies, *The Silent House* and *Splinters in the Navy*; *Mary*, the German version of Hitchcock's *Murder* (spotted playing on East German television!); and, as mentioned above, at least some of the reels of Forde's *Ghost Train*.

Experience tells us that more than a handful of the films we have quoted will be languishing somewhere, and we appeal to vault managers, collectors, laboratories, colleague archives abroad, and all our friends in the industry to unlock their cupboards and scour their shelves. Even if all we come up with on a title is a 16 mm print saved by a collector in Kentucky, it will be supremely better than nothing. And one word of warning: time is not on our side where nitrate film is concerned, and prints on this stock will inevitably decay and disintegrate in a very few years.

This is the first time the National Film Archive has initiated a public search for Britain's lost films. If it is successful – and with the media's help it can be – our somewhat ravaged national moving image heritage will be that much richer and more complete.

CLYDE JEAVONS *Curator, National Film Archive*

THE FILM-MAKERS

Walter Forde

Walter Forde (left) directs Jack Hulbert and Cicely Courtneidge in *The Ghost Train*

'If Britain had a silent comedian who could justifiably be placed beside the American Big Four, it would undoubtedly be Walter Forde,' wrote Ivan Butler in *Silent Magic: Rediscovering the Silent Film Era* (1987), adding '. . . he made his film debut in a series of shorts in 1921, and soon became known for his hallmark, a be-ribboned straw hat, and for his character of a normal, well-meaning young man who lands himself in endless difficulties. He may have been influenced by Harold Lloyd, but his style is distinctive.'

Full-length comedies had not been attempted in Britain until Forde starred in and directed his first two features, *Wait and See* and *What Next?*, which appeared in 1928. He then abandoned acting (other than guest appearances in many of his films) and concentrated on directing thrillers, comedies and comedy thrillers, becoming one of the leading lights of British film-making in the 1930s and working with stars like Conrad Veidt, Jack Hulbert, Arthur Askey and Sid Field.

Forde's best-known work as a director includes *The Ghost Train* (both the 1931 and 1941 versions), *Rome Express* (1932), *Chu Chin Chow* and *Jack Ahoy* (both 1934), *Bulldog Jack* and *King of the Damned* (both 1935), *Cheer Boys Cheer* (1939, often described as the prototype of 'Ealing comedy'), and *Cardboard Cavalier* (1948).

Work that is missing, believed lost: *What Next?* (1928); *The Last Hour*, *Lord Richard in the Pantry* and *Bed and Breakfast* (all 1930); *The Ghost Train* (1931 version); *Condemned to Death* and *Lord Babs* (both 1932).

Ralph Ince

Ralph Ince has been overshadowed by his brother Thomas. But Ralph was an important director and actor in the silent period. On the basis of some surviving early films as director – *Strength of Men* and *His Last Fight* (both 1913), *The Right Girl?* and *The Phantom Sweetheart* (both 1915) – he has been pinpointed by Barry Salt ('The Unknown Ince', *Sight and Sound*, Autumn 1988) as 'the first master of mainstream continuity cinema, or "classical cinema", or whatever one wants to call the standard form of cinema which everyone accepts as normal'.

In the early 1930s he was an actor (in films like *Little Caesar*, *The Star Witness*, *The*

Roy William Neill, Ralph
Ince and Irving Asher

Lost Squadron and *The Hatchet Man*) as much as a director (of films such as *Lucky Devils*). In Britain he co-starred with Marion Marsh in *Love at Second Sight* (1933) and directed and acted in several 'quota quickie' productions for various companies. But his principal association was with Warner Bros First National at Teddington, where he directed sixteen films. He also appeared in several of them and in Monty Banks's *So You Won't Talk!* (1935). His speciality was crime pictures, mostly dramas, occasionally comedies. According to Salt, 'Only two of his films from this period survive, and they are solidly made, very good-looking productions, appreciably better than the usual idea of British "quota quickies".' These are *Crime Unlimited* (1935) and *The Perfect Crime* (1937).

Ince died at 50, following a car crash outside the Albert Hall on 11 April 1937, a week before he was to begin directing another film for Warner Bros.

The missing Teddington films are: *No Escape*, *A Glimpse of Paradise* and *What's in a Name?* (all 1934); *Murder at Monte Carlo*, *Mr What's His Name?* and *Black Mask* (all 1935); *Gaol Break*, *Twelve Good Men*, *Fair Exchange* and *Hail and Farewell* (all 1936); and *The Vulture*, *Side Street Angel*, *It's Not Cricket* and *The Man Who Made Diamonds* (all 1937).

Max Miller

Born in 1895, Max Miller made his reputation with ribald material in the music hall, earning himself the sobriquet 'The Cheeky Chappie'. He played supporting parts in *The Good Companions*, *Channel Crossing* and *Friday the Thirteenth* (all 1933), *Princess Charming* (1934), and *Things Are Looking Up* (1935). Then Warner Bros First National decided to feature him in *Get Off My Foot* (1935) and *Educated Evans* (1936), both now missing. Their success led to a series of films at the Teddington studios, of which *Don't Get Me Wrong* (1937), *Everything Happens to Me* (1938) and *Hoots Mon* (1939) are known to survive, while *Transatlantic Trouble/Take It from Me* (1937), *Thank Evans* (1938) and *The Good Old Days* (1939) are believed lost. Miller had just started another film at Teddington, *Hold Your Hats*, under the direction of Joseph Henabery, when war was declared and it was abandoned. He made one further big screen appearance, starring in *Asking for Trouble* (1943) for British National.

Roy William Neill
directing Polly Ward
and Max Miller in *Thank
Evans*. Cameraman
Basil Emmott in pensive
mood behind Neill

Roy William Neill

Born in 1886 on a ship off the coast of Ireland, Roy William Neill was an accomplished director of genre movies who began his career in 1915 working for Thomas H. Ince and directed his own first film in 1916. He made dozens of American films, including *The Viking* (1929) and *The Black Room* (1935), before coming to Britain, where he directed *Dr Syn* (1937) with George Arliss and thirteen films for Warner Bros First National between 1936 and 1939, of which ten are missing, believed lost: *Gypsy* (1937); *Quiet Please, Simply Terrific, The Viper, Double or Quits* and *Thank Evans* (all 1938); and *A Gentleman's Gentleman, The Good Old Days, Murder Will Out* and *His Brother's Keeper* (all 1939). Neill then returned to Hollywood, where he directed most of the Sherlock Holmes adventures starring Basil Rathbone and such films as *Frankenstein Meets the Wolf Man, Gypsy Wildcat* and *Black Angel*. He died in 1946.

Michael Powell

It was in 1931, when American distributors in Britain were commissioning supporting films at £1 per foot, solely in order to meet quota requirements and virtually regardless of quality, that the twenty-six-year-old Michael Powell was able to start directing featurettes, made with producer Jerome J. Jackson for their own company, Film Engineering. Only one of the company's five films directed by Powell is known to survive – *Rynox* (1931). A Jerry Verno comedy that followed, *Hotel Splendide* (1932), happily exists, but three films that Powell and Jackson made under the banner of Westminster Films have disappeared. The net result is that only two of Powell's first nine films as a director have been located.

Many subsequent films are also lost from the period before Powell achieved the

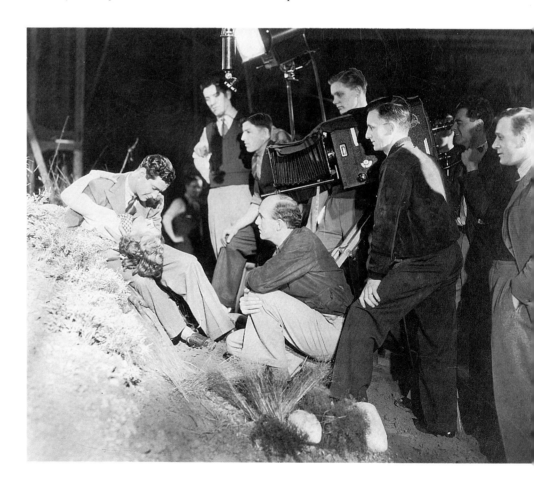

freedom to make his first major work, *The Edge of the World* (1937). These early efforts are doubtless of greatly varying aesthetic value, but the surviving examples show a technical inventiveness and an attempt to circumvent the restrictions of genre and budget that make them both interesting and entertaining. Michael Powell's lost films are: *Two Crowded Hours* (1931), *My Friend the King* (1931), *The Rasp* (1931), *The Star Reporter* (1931), *C.O.D.* (1932), *His Lordship* (1932), *Born Lucky* (1932), *The Girl in the Crowd* (1934), *The Price of a Song* (1935), *Some Day* (1935), *The Brown Wallet* (1936), *The Man Behind the Mask* (1936).

Bernard Vorhaus

Born in New York in 1904. Following script work in Hollywood, Bernard Vorhaus visited Britain for a holiday in the late 1920s and stayed until 1937, directing eleven features – comedies, dramas, musicals and thrillers – for the burgeoning British quota quickie industry. His skill as a director won the admiration of editor David Lean, who cut two of his films, including the lost *Money for Speed*. In 'Vorhaus: A Director Rediscovered' (*Sight and Sound*, Winter 1986–7), Geoff Brown noted: 'Working at levels of the British film industry where time and money were scarce but trivial material grew like weeds, Vorhaus persistently pumped cinematic life into his projects. Other quota directors, pressed for time, positioned their characters on the drawing-room sofa, shouted the misnomer "Action!" and let the dialogue work its poison. Vorhaus varied the scene with elaborate set-ups, tracking shots, cut-in vignettes, angled compositions – anything that would turn the script into a movie, not 6,000 feet of celluloid churned out to fulfil a legal obligation.'

Vorhaus was rediscovered in National Film Archive tributes at the 1986 Edinburgh Film Festival, at the Museum of Modern Art in New York and at the

Cinémathèque Française in Paris, followed by a season of his work at the National Film Theatre in December 1986 when surviving British films such as *The Ghost Camera* and *Crime on the Hill* (both 1933) and *The Last Journey* (1935) were shown to appreciative audiences. After 1937, Vorhaus returned to America, where he directed lower-rung films of occasional accomplishment like *Mr District Attorney in the Carter Case* (1941), *Affairs of Jimmy Valentine* (1942) and *The Amazing Mr X* (or *The Spiritualist*) (1948) before his career was terminated by the blacklist. He soon returned to Britain, where he has lived ever since.

Films missing: *On Thin Ice* and *Money for Speed* (1933); *Blind Justice* (1934); and *Dark World* (1935).

Bernard Vorhaus (bearded, front row right) with (back row) composer Charles Cowlrick, star/writer Hugh Brooke, publicist Geoff Davies, a visitor, Leslie Landau; and (front row) a visitor, dance director Hedley Briggs and Tamara Desni on the set of *Dark World*

Arthur Woods

Arthur Woods

Arthur Woods's career ended tragically with his death in action in the Second World War at the age of 38. Best known today for the superb thriller *They Drive By Night* (1939), with Emlyn Williams and Ernest Thesiger, he was a former editor, assistant director and writer who became a director in 1933 and made more than two dozen, mostly low-budget, films in less than eight years. He established his reputation at BIP and first worked for Warner Bros First National at Teddington on the well-received *Where's Sally?* (1936). Including *Where's Sally?*, eleven of his Teddington films are missing. The others are: *Irish for Luck* (1936); *Mayfair Melody*, *The Windmill*, *The Compulsory Wife* and *You Live and Learn* (1937); *The Dark Stairway*, *The Singing Cop*, *Thistledown* and *Dangerous Medicine* (1938); and *Confidential Lady* (1939).

THE FILMS

1914

A Study in Scarlet

Director	George Pearson
Leading players	James Bragington
	Fred Paul
	Agnes Glynne
	Harry Paulo
Screenwriter	Harry Engholm (from the novel by Sir Arthur Conan Doyle)
Cinematographer	Walter Buckstone
Producer	G. B. Samuelson
Production company	Samuelson
Distributor	Moss
Length	5,749 ft

The first Sherlock Holmes film made in Britain and the first screen version of the first Holmes story. Delayed by the outbreak of war, it was released in Britain at the same time as an unauthorised two-reeler by Universal came out in America, directed by and starring Francis Ford (brother of John).

The British version was feature-length and devoted most of its footage to the Mormon episode of the story which leads years later to the murder in London investigated by Holmes, whose first appearance is not until late in the picture. The Mormon wagon train sequences were filmed on an epic scale, sand dunes at Southport representing the plains of Salt Lake and hundreds of locals being recruited to portray the pioneers. Cheddar Gorge stood in for the Rockies. Holmes was played by James Bragington, an employee of the production company's Birmingham office who had never acted before but who was cast on the basis of his gaunt appearance (it was his first and last film).

Pictures and the Picturegoer reported: 'Those who see the fine Samuelson film of *A Study in Scarlet* cannot help but admire Fred Paul's powerful rendering of Jefferson Hope, the leading character. One is filled with regret when the long film comes to an end, not only because of its ingenious story, but also because Mr Paul's intense acting succeeds throughout in gripping and fascinating his audience.'

James Bragington as Sherlock Holmes in *A Study in Scarlet*

James Bragington as Sherlock Holmes examines the evidence at the scene of the crime in *A Study in Scarlet*

Locals gathered on Southport Sands to play Mormon pioneers in *A Study in Scarlet*

1916

Ultus, the Man from the Dead

US titles	*Ultus 1: The Townsend Mystery,* *Ultus 2: The Ambassador's Diamond*
Director/screenwriter	George Pearson
Leading players	Aurele Sydney J. L. V. Leigh A. Caton Woodville Marjorie Dunbar M. Goujet
Production company/ distributor	Gaumont
Length	6,147 ft

Aurele Sydney (right) in the title role of *Ultus, The Man from the Dead*

Following the enormous success of the *Fantômas* films in France, Léon Gaumont instructed George Pearson, as newly appointed production chief at Gaumont's Lime Grove studios in London, to create an avenger character who would appeal as much to British audiences. Pearson responded with Ultus (from the Latin *Ultor*, an avenger), a diamond miner robbed and left to die in the Australian desert by a treacherous partner. Five years later, Ultus returns to exact an elaborate revenge on his old partner, now a wealthy and respected baronet and patron of the arts. A sympathetic and admiring detective is on the trail of Ultus.

An unknown French-Australian called Aurele Sydney was selected by Léon Gaumont to play Ultus. In an effort to speed up the action, Pearson experimented with inserting titles as the actors began to speak, returning for the last lip movement, instructing them to convey their state of mind by their facial expression before the titles came up.

This film was a huge success throughout the world, even in France, and Pearson wrote and directed three sequels: *Ultus and the Grey Lady* (1916), *Ultus and the Secret of the Night* (1916), and *Ultus and the Three-Button Mystery* (1917).

'The Ultus films . . . were out-and-out thrillers and among the most important of the period . . . they were crowded with more "punches" per reel than many more lurid films, and yet had well constructed plots with none of the incongruities and absurdities with which less skilful writers enlivened their slender stories' (Rachael Low, *The History of the British Film 1914–1918*).

1916

She

H. Rider Haggard's adventure story about explorers in Egypt discovering a lost city ruled by a 500-year-old queen – with one of the explorers proving to be the reincarnation of her lover of ancient times – had been filmed already in America by Edison in 1908 and Thanhouser in 1911. The bold British pioneer Will Barker made the first British and first feature-length version with French star Alice Delysia. This was one of the few British films of its period to have lavish settings, for which a designer was specially hired, and to feature huge crowd scenes.

Directors	Will Barker, Horace Lisle Lucoque
Leading players	Alice Delysia Henry Victor Sydney Bland Blanche Forsythe Jack Denton J. Hastings Batson
Screenwriter	Nellie E. Lucoque (from the novel by H. Rider Haggard)
Designer	Lancelot Speed
Producer	Will Barker
Production company	Barker Motion Photography, in association with Horace Lisle Lucoque and Charles B. Cochran
Distributor	Lucoque
Length	5,400 ft

Alice Delysia in two scenes from *She*

1916

Director   Thomas Bentley

Leading players   Isobel Elsom
Owen Nares
Campbell Gullan
Minna Grey
Mary Lincoln
Hubert Harben
Esme Hubbard
Cecil Morton York

Screenwriter   Harry Engholm (from the play by Arnold Bennett and Edward Knoblock)

Production company   Samuelson

Distributor   Moss

Length   8,640 ft

Campbell Gullan and Mary Lincoln in *Milestones*

Milestones

A spectacular historical drama – the story of several generations of shipbuilders who are radical in their youth and become reactionary in their old age. *The Bioscope* noted that as part of its depiction of changing eras 'we behold Dickens and Disraeli walking the streets of old London; Queen Victoria with Prince Albert at the launch of the first ironclad; a wonderful old omnibus and the first motor-car, the latter with its flag-man walking solemnly in front; an ancient high bicycle; the first telephone and the first typewriter; not to mention a typical modern picture theatre.'

Thomas Bentley was especially noted for his adaptations of Charles Dickens and remained a significant director in the 1930s, when his work included *Those Were the Days* (1934), his third version of *The Old Curiosity Shop* (1935) and the Sherlock Holmes adventure *Silver Blaze* (1937).

1923

**Director/
screenwriter/producer**   George Pearson

Leading players   Betty Balfour
Harry Jonas
Frank Stanmore
Annie Esmond
Nancy Price
Sydney Fairbrother
Eric Smith

Cinematographers   Percy Strong (London night scenes),
A. H. Blake

Production company   Welsh-Pearson

Distributor   Gaumont

Length   6,290 ft

Love, Life and Laughter

Having scored an enormous success with the first *Squibs* comedies and made a leading star out of Betty Balfour, George Pearson placed her in a more ambitious film in which he experimented with narrative structure, mixing fantasy and realism. Balfour portrayed a chorus girl dreaming of success who falls in love with a struggling young author. Pearson set up his final scene at the start, then told the story leading up to it, averting a tragic conclusion by revealing it all to have been a story imagined by the writer.

In his autobiography, *Flashback* (1957), Pearson recalls various ingenious means by which he overcame a limited budget: creating the illusion of factory machinery with the shadow of the moving parts of a clock, conveying an open-air night-time dance with a searchlight and highly-placed camera, and using a drifting balloon to suggest the great height of a tenement staircase.

The British press gave the film some rave notices. *Manchester Guardian*: 'George Pearson has all the talent of the British screen in his head and hands. Devotees have called it his masterpiece, and so it is.' *The Times*: 'Mr George Pearson has told his story with the utmost cunning, and brings it to a shining and unexpected climax. Miss Balfour once again proves she is the cleverest comedienne now playing in British films.' *Evening News*: '. . . the most ambitious thing Welsh-Pearson have done. It leaves the American film with no advantage technically, and the settings are much more elaborate than are usually seen in British pictures. As for Miss Balfour . . . what few people there are who have not fallen beneath the spell of her pretty face, clever comedy, and sympathetic interpretation of human feelings must surely be captured now.'

The film bears no relation to the 1934 Gracie Fields picture of the same title.

Betty Balfour in *Love, Life and Laughter*

1923

Lily of the Alley

Director/screenwriter	Henry Edwards
Leading players	Henry Edwards
	Chrissie White
	Campbell Gullan
	Mary Brough
	Frank Stanmore
	Lionel d'Aragon
Cinematographer	Charles Bryce
Production company/ distributor	Hepworth
Length	6,590 ft

Henry Edwards was an important actor, director, producer and writer who made more than a dozen films for the Hepworth company. He directed and acted opposite his wife, the popular star Chrissie White, in *Lily of the Alley*.

In this film, Edwards boldly dispensed with the usual inter-titles to convey dialogue and information. It was a Cockney love story in which Edwards portrayed a man who gives up drinking when he marries and runs a coffee stall with a friend (Frank Stanmore). His eyesight begins to fail and his long working hours make his wife (Chrissie White) brood. She dreams that he goes blind and is murdered by a robber who takes his savings. An operation fully restores his eyesight and the couple start a new life in the country.

Chrissie White and Henry Edwards in *Lily of the Alley*

The Bioscope commented at length on Edwards' 'stimulating artistic experiment', noting that the elimination of titles made for less disruptive viewing but giving examples of scenes in which the words being spoken were awkwardly conveyed by miming, gestures and inserts when a concise title card would have been much simpler. 'In their present form [certain scenes] do not give one the feeling, as they should, that the producer has chosen the clearest and most direct means of expression, but rather that he is struggling, a trifle laboriously, against a self-imposed handicap. As an entertainment, *Lily of the Alley* is an excellent piece of work in a school of which Mr Edwards has already proved himself a master. Its outstanding feature is the richly human Cockney characterisation of Mr Edwards himself, as the light-hearted hero who is sobered so effectively by marriage; of Chrissie White as the hunted slum girl; of Frank Stanmore as the ebullient Alf; and of Mary Brough as a generous-natured widow. As a vehicle for these delightful low-life studies, the story, in itself rather thin and commonplace, admirably serves its purpose, though one feels that a suitable dramatic climax might have been devised without recourse to the over-worked dream ending.'

Reveille

Director/	
screenwriter/producer	George Pearson
Leading players	Betty Balfour
	Stewart Rome
	Ralph Forbes
	Sydney Fairbrother
	Frank Stanmore
	Guy Phillips
Cinematographer	Percy Strong
Art directors	Leslie Dawson,
	Harry Jonas
Production company	Welsh-Pearson
Distributor	Gaumont
Length	8,400 ft

Pearson followed *Love, Life and Laughter* with two more farces in the *Squibs* series. 'But now Pearson was becoming more ambitious and in 1924 wrote and produced one of his more important pictures, *Reveille*, in which he attempted to show a slice of life rather than a plot. This . . . was a diffuse story of how the war had affected a group of humble people, and dealt with a large number of characters in two periods in an anecdotal manner rather than the closely woven plot of the time. Pearson was proud of the film, and attached much importance to the fact that he had deliberately set out to express a theme, which he described as the Victory of Courage, rather than tell a story. Although the film was felt to be a little slow, the mood of sentimental patriotism suited the temper of the time and it was extremely success-ful both at the box office and with the critics.' (Rachael Low, *The History of the British Film 1918–1929*.)

Betty Balfour played a woman whose brother (Guy Phillips) and lover (Ralph Forbes) are killed in the war. She works as a seamstress to keep herself and her small son, and helps an unemployed ex-soldier (Stewart Rome) overcome the despair that is turning him into a left-wing revolutionary. One of Pearson's most daring ideas was to show the full two minutes of remembrance for the dead on 11 November, with the camera focusing the whole time on a widow (Henrietta Watson) who has lost all three of her sons in the war. She is shown looking out of a window, the only movement being the stirring of a lace curtain in the wind. Even the musical accompaniment halted for the two minutes.

Ralph Forbes and Betty Balfour in *Reveille*

Stewart Rome, Betty Balfour, Walter Tennyson, Ralph Forbes and Frank Stanmore in *Reveille*

1926

The Mountain Eagle

German title	*Der Bergadler*
US title	*Fear o' God*
Director	Alfred Hitchcock
Leading players	Nita Naldi Bernard Goetzke Malcolm Keen John Hamilton
Screenwriter	Eliot Stannard
Cinematographer	Baron Ventimiglia
Art directors	Willy Reiber, Ludwig Reiber
Production companies	Gainsborough/ Münchener Lichtspielkunst
Distributor	W & F
Length	7,503 ft

Alfred Hitchcock at work on *The Mountain Eagle*. Behind his shoulder his future wife, scriptgirl Alma Reville

Five scene stills from *The Mountain Eagle* (continued on p. 26)

This is the only feature by Britain's best-known film-maker that is no longer known to exist. It was the second film that Alfred Hitchcock directed – after *The Pleasure Garden* – and, like that film, was an Anglo-German production based at studios in Munich. Location work was done in the Tyrol.

The story concerns a young schoolmistress driven into the mountains after rejecting the attentions of the local justice of the peace. She is given shelter by a mysterious recluse who marries her to stop scandal and who is jailed on a trumped-up murder charge.

Hitchcock himself was dismissive. 'It was a very bad movie,' he told François Truffaut. 'The producers were always trying to break into the American market, so they wanted another film star. And so, for the part of the village schoolmistress, they sent me Nita Naldi, the successor to Theda Bara. She had fingernails out to there. Ridiculous!'

The Mountain Eagle

The reviewer in *The Bioscope* agreed that 'the story is lacking in conviction' but declared it was 'of interest because of skilful direction and good acting', referring to 'the undoubted artistic merits of the production' and 'at times brilliant direction'. The scene stills that survive are particularly tantalising.

1928

The Constant Nymph

Director	Adrian Brunel
Leading players	Ivor Novello Mabel Poulton Benita Hume Frances Doble Mary Clare J. H. Roberts
Screenwriters	Adrian Brunel, Alma Reville, Margaret Kennedy (from the play by Margaret Kennedy and Basil Dean, based on the novel by Margaret Kennedy)
Cinematographer	Dave Gobbett
Producers	Basil Dean, Michael Balcon
Production company	Gainsborough
Distributor	W & F
Length	10,600 ft

Margaret Kennedy's novel, about a composer who leaves his domineering rich wife for a young woman with a serious heart condition, became a successful play in 1926 and was filmed three times. The missing first version, directed by Adrian Brunel, was a considerable success.

Ivor Novello and Mabel Poulton in *The Constant Nymph*

Ivan Butler in *Cinema in Britain* (1973) wrote that the silent film was: 'Notable for a most delightful performance by Mabel Poulton, an actress of great charm whose career was to be so shortly terminated by the advent of sound, for which her accent was unsuitable. Novello, opposite her, is also at his best as the conventionally tempestuous musician: his big moment is when, after careful coaching, he conducts a full-scale orchestra at the Queen's Hall in a totally soundless symphony. Though the film was accused of sticking too closely to the stage play, there is some beautiful location work in the Austrian Tyrol and the action – unlike that of many such transfers – is never slow.'

Co-producer Basil Dean directed the 1934 version with Brian Aherne and Victoria Hopper. The rights to the play and novel were acquired by Warner Bros, for whom Edmund Goulding directed the 1943 version starring Charles Boyer and Joan Fontaine, best noted for its Erich Wolfgang Korngold score. Although both these later versions survive, they are rarely if ever seen because the rights to the source material have expired.

What Next?

Director	Walter Forde
Leading players	Walter Forde
	Pauline Johnson
	Frank Stanmore
	Douglas Payne
Screenwriters	Walter Forde,
	Harry Fowler Mear
Cinematographer	Geoffrey Faithfull
Art director	W. G. Saunders
Editor	Walter Forde
Producer	Archibald Nettlefold
Production company	Nettlefold
Distributor	Butcher's Film Service
Length	6,170 ft

Frank Stanmore and
Walter Forde in *What
Next?*

Frank Stanmore,
Pauline Johnson and
Walter Forde in *What
Next?*

Opposite: Walter
Forde
in *What Next?*

What Next? was a farce in which Walter Forde played a salesman who buys a valuable antique candlestick as a present for his girlfriend (Pauline Johnson), only to engage the murderous attentions of a deranged collector (Douglas Payne), who imagines himself to be Napoleon and who has scoured the world seeking this particular object.

The Bioscope commented: 'This is light, irresponsible farce in which the plot is nothing and everything depends on the ingenuity and novelty of the situations, and the slick smartness with which they are reeled off from start to finish. The whole thing goes with a swing, and if there is no outstanding feature, there is no lack of entertainment . . . Hectic chases and much rush-about comedy acts are very cleverly put over, and the quality is excellent.'

Lord Richard in the Pantry

Director	Walter Forde
Leading players	Richard Cooper Dorothy Seacombe Marjorie Hume
Screenwriters	Harry Fowler Mear, (uncredited additions) Sidney Gilliat (from the 1919 play by Sydney Blow and Douglas Hoare based on the novel by Martin Swayne)
Cinematographer	Sidney Blythe
Art director	James Carter
Editor	Jack Harris
Producers	Julius Hagen, Henry Edwards
Production company	Twickenham Film Studio
Distributor	Warner Bros
Running time	83 mins

From *The Bioscope*: 'Extremely funny tribulations of a noodle aristocrat, who, dreading arrest through the failure of a company, acts as butler in his own mansion. . . . If the leading character is not comic in the clown sense, he is something better, being the personification of incapacity and amiability, perpetually suffering from muddled bewilderment. Though his misadventures are hardly to be viewed as possible, the acting by the star and supporting cast is so good, the incidents so delightfully absurd, and much of the dialogue so entertaining that there are no dull moments. The director deserves praise for sound construction, the avoidance of padding and good continuity. Yet it is a pity he allows the brilliant comedy of the early scenes to degenerate into farce, and finish in the realm of rush-about nonsense.'

Richard Cooper and
Leo Sheffield in *Lord
Richard in the Pantry*

And *Variety* declared: 'This one is distinctly over the level of the average British talker . . . Recording and photography very good, and a travelling microphone makes good use of a crazy directors' meeting for smart technical effects. . . . Richard Cooper has his usual silly fop role as the hero, and stutters his accentuated lines effectively.'

Richard Cooper was a busy performer in British films from 1929 to 1935, returning to the screen in *Shipyard Sally* (1939). He starred in two other missing films by Walter Forde, *The Last Hour* and *Bed and Breakfast*.

1930

The Last Hour

Director/editor	Walter Forde
Leading players	Stewart Rome
	Richard Cooper
	Kathleen Vaughan
Screenwriter	Harry Fowler Mear
	(from the play by
	Charles Bennett)
Cinematographer	Geoffrey Faithfull
Art director	W. G. Saunders
Producer	Archibald Nettlefold
Production company	Nettlefold
Distributor	Butcher's Film Service
Running time	77 mins

The first all-talkie produced at Nettlefold's Walton-on-Thames studios was the film version of a successful play by Charles Bennett which had opened in December 1928. It marked comedian Walter Forde's decision to concentrate on directing, with only fleeting guest appearances in his films.

The Last Hour was described by *The Bioscope* as 'an exciting story concerning the theft of secret plans for the production of a fatal death ray by the agents of a foreign power, and their subsequent discomfiture by members of the Secret Service . . . The earnest performance of an excellent company does much to gloss over the rather palpable improbabilities of the situation.' Stewart Rome was the villainous Prince Nicola de Kovatch, who uses the death ray to threaten British ships and aircraft.

Stewart Rome, Richard Cooper and unidentified performer in *The Last Hour*

1930

Bed and Breakfast

Director	Walter Forde
Leading players	Richard Cooper
	Jane Baxter
	David Hawthorne
	Sari Maritza
	Cyril McLaglen
	Alf Goddard
Screenwriters	Harry Fowler Mear,
	(uncredited additions)
	Sidney Gilliat (from the
	play by Frederick
	Whitney)
Cinematographer	William Shenton
Art director	Andrew Mazzei
Producer	L'Estrange Fawcett
Production company/	
distributor	Gaumont-British
Running time	68 mins

Richard Cooper, unidentified performer, Frederick Volpe, Muriel Aked, Jane Baxter (back view) and unidentified performer in *Bed and Breakfast*

Bed and Breakfast

In this farcical comedy, a married couple quarrel because the husband has been photographed with another woman. The husband and the other woman go off together to teach the wife a lesson, and the wife goes out with the other woman's fiancé to teach her husband a lesson. They run into each other at a country retreat, where they are joined by a clergyman and his wife and by a bookie and his family, all having missed the last train, and by a pair of burglars who are each suspected of being the wife's lover.

The Bioscope remarked: 'There is nothing original in this story, yet, nevertheless, there are a series of comedy gags which will thoroughly amuse popular audiences. . . . Walter Forde has managed to keep the action going with plenty of semi-coarse back-chat from the bookmaker and occasional lamentations from the clergyman and his straight-laced wife. The climax, with the police deciding that the parson is the ringleader of the gang they are after, is a fitting one to a night of errors and discomfort.'

1931   *The Ghost Train*

Director	Walter Forde
Leading players	Jack Hulbert
	Cicely Courtneidge
	Donald Calthrop
	Angela Baddeley
	Cyril Raymond
	Ann Todd
Screenwriters	Angus MacPhail,
	Lajos Biró,
	(additional dialogue)
	Sidney Gilliat (based on
	the 1925 play by
	Arnold Ridley)
Cinematographer	Leslie Rowson
Art director	Walter W. Murton
Editor	Ian Dalrymple
Producers	Michael Balcon,
	(associate)
	Philip Samuel
Production company	Gainsborough
Distributor	W & F
Running time	72 mins

Opposite: Ann Todd,
Cicely Courtneidge,
unidentified performer
and Jack Hulbert in *The
Ghost Train*

All is not lost. Five reels of picture and two reels of soundtrack of *The Ghost Train* do survive in the National Film Archive – but this makes the absence of the rest all the more frustrating.

This is the story of an assorted group of railway passengers stranded overnight at a station said to be haunted, but the ghost train turns out to be a real train operated by gun runners. The film made screen stars out of stage performers Jack Hulbert and Cicely Courtneidge, previously seen by picturegoers only in an extract from a show in *Elstree Calling* (1930). Walter Forde himself appeared as one of the passengers. The impressive exterior work involved the construction of a railway station on a side line of the Great Western near Bath.

The Bioscope declared: 'Amazingly good "screenisation" of Arnold Ridley's mystery play. . . . The story opens on a moving train and Jack Hulbert's nonsense begins. Skilfully handled comedy creates the impression that there is not a foot of waste film from beginning to end. In the waiting room there is some of the funniest stuff ever put over by any artist, British or foreign. And the atmosphere of mystery and brooding uneasiness, contrasted with the "damn the ghost idea" attitude of Jack Hulbert as the "silly ass" detective, is amazingly cleverly contrived. With a deft touch Walter Forde has guided his artists through a none too convincing story, extracting from it every ounce of credulous virtue; every gasp of dramatic intensity. The result is one of the most gripping British films ever produced.'

The Ghost Train had a profitable week's engagement in February 1933 at the celebrated Roxy Theater, the world's largest cinema, in New York City.

The story was later parodied in the classic Will Hay comedy *Oh! Mr. Porter* (1937), and was re-made in 1941 as a vehicle for Arthur Askey.

Arnold Ridley's play and this Gainsborough film version attracted foreign film-makers: Geza von Bolvary made the first silent version of the play in Germany in 1927 and Lajos Lázár made a Hungarian version of the 1931 film (released in 1933), keeping all the more distant shots and reshooting the others, and replacing the British cast with popular Hungarian performers. A print of this is held by the National Film Archive.

1931

Director	Michael Powell
Leading players	John Longden
	Jane Welsh
	Jerry Verno
	Michael Hogan
Screenwriter	Jefferson Farjeon
Cinematographer	Geoffrey Faithfull
Art director	C. Saunders
Editor	John Seabourne
Producers	Jerry Jackson,
	Henry Cohen
Production company	Film Engineering
Distributor	Fox
Running time	43 mins

John Longden, Michael
Hogan and Jane Welsh
in *Two Crowded
Hours*

Two Crowded Hours

Two Crowded Hours

Michael Powell's first film as a director, this murder mystery featured John Longden (the policeman hero of Hitchcock's *Blackmail*) as a detective seeking an escaped convict, with Jane Welsh as the tec's girlfriend who is in danger because it was her evidence that put the criminal behind bars. Jerry Verno scored a hit as a taxi driver with a line in Cockney wit and caustic repartee. After one of his fares is murdered, he helps the detective in his search.

The film was shot in twelve days in April 1931 and Powell enlivened the story with carefully chosen locations – including a taxi driver's shelter in North London and street scenes in Upper Rathbone Street near Oxford Street – scheduling filming for when the natural light was most suitable.

In his autobiography, *A Life in Movies*, Powell recalled: '*Two Crowded Hours* was obviously influenced by Continental films. There were lots of clever angles and quick-cutting, but it was also obvious that the director meant to entertain first and foremost. The shocks and suspense were of the most primitive kind, but they worked . . . The climax of the film comes when the villain tries to murder the heroine, who is rescued by John Longden in the nick of time. The villain runs out into the road and is run down and killed by Jerry Verno's taxi. John Seabourne and I, working hand in hand, achieved a bang-up finish with a kaleidoscopic montage of images inspired by the Soviet cinema.'

Two Crowded Hours was well-received. 'This little picture is a skilful blend of tragedy and comedy,' declared *The Bioscope*. 'Just a quota quickie, but much better than many more ambitious pictures turned out this side,' reported *Variety*'s London correspondent. The film ran six weeks in the West End, supporting one of Fox's big Hollywood films at the Tivoli in the Strand. For Powell, this was an encouraging start to a succession of low-budget pictures, including several with Jerry Verno.

The final scene from
Two Crowded Hours

The Bells

Directors	Oscar M. Werndorff, Harcourt Templeman
Leading players	Donald Calthrop Jane Welsh Edward Sinclair
Screenwriter	C. H. Dand (from the 1869 French play *Le Juif polonais* by Alexandre Chatrian and Emile Erckmann)
Cinematographers	Günther Krampf, Eric Cross
Editors	Lars Moen, Michael Hankinson
Music	Gustav Holst
Supervisor	Sergei Nolbandov
Production company	British Sound Film Productions (BSFP)
Distributor	PDC
Running time	75 mins

Several versions of this story, in which Henry Irving made his first sensational success, had already appeared as silents, including a 1925 Hollywood adaptation starring Lionel Barrymore.

This sound version was trilingual. Co-director Oscar (or Otto) Werndorff had been the chief architect of the last Emperor of Austria and is better known as the art director of such celebrated films as *Variété* (1925) and Hitchcock's *The 39 Steps* (1935), *Secret Agent* and *Sabotage* (both 1936). Austrian cinematographer Günther Krampf had photographed such films as *Die Büchse der Pandora* (*Pandora's Box*, 1929) before coming to England, where he also shot *Rome Express* (1932), *The Tunnel* (1935) and many others. *The Bells*, which included scenes shot in the Grampians during a howling blizzard and very heavy snows in March 1931, was his first work in Britain and he regarded it as among the best he had done. The score was by Gustav Holst – the first time a notable composer had consented to compose incidental music for a British talking picture. His contribution included the 'Storm Prelude', the 'Wedding Feast', dance music and drinking songs.

In this psychological thriller, Donald Calthrop portrayed the proprietor of a small inn in Alsace. Struggling to provide for his wife and daughter, he murders a Polish Jew for his belt of gold and flings the body down a precipice. Years later, the prosperous innkeeper, now burgomaster, is unnerved when a young police sergeant (Edward Sinclair) arrives to re-open investigations into the death of the Jew and falls in love with the innkeeper's daughter (Jane Welsh). The innkeeper becomes psychologically unhinged at his daughter's wedding, particularly by the sound of bells, and he confesses to the murder before killing himself.

Surviving stills suggest the visual distinctiveness of the film, but some of the touches were not appreciated by *The Bioscope*'s reviewer, who commented that 'some eccentricities of lighting and grouping rob important scenes of dignity and

Donald Calthrop in
The Bells

dramatic effect. The row of guests who listen to the confession of Mathias [Calthrop], like figures from Madame Tussaud's, by eccentricity of lighting, come dangerously near to the grotesque.' But he added: 'Some of the settings are extremely picturesque and the exteriors well photographed.'

Picturegoer found the film 'entirely artificial and very slow in action', adding, 'To some extent, this is counteracted by very clever camera work, which includes various kaleidoscopic effects, rapid "blackouts", and a general tendency to follow the lines of German technique.'

It was not the kind of film to succeed with average British audiences and the production company was soon out of business.

1931

Director	Michael Powell
Leading players	Jerry Verno
	Robert Holmes
	Eric Pavitt
	Phyllis Loring
	Tracey Holmes
Screenwriter	Jefferson Farjeon
Cinematographer	Geoffrey Faithfull
Art director	C. Saunders
Editor	John Seabourne
Producer	Jerry Jackson
Production company	Film Engineering
Distributor	Fox
Running time	47 mins

My Friend the King

The further adventures of Jerry Verno's Cockney cab driver from *Two Crowded Hours*. Once again he is involved in crime when a fare-paying passenger comes to harm. He arrives at a mansion where the young heir to a throne is living in style, attended by fancily attired servants. The boy and the cabbie become friends, and the latter dresses up as a demure countess to help foil a kidnap attempt by revolutionaries.

In *Powell, Pressburger and Others* (BFI, 1978), Michael Powell recalled: 'It was a very weak story about a little boy who was some foreign king staying in London and got kidnapped. I only remember it as a complete failure.' *The Bioscope* agreed: 'A better vehicle should have been devised for a comedian of such ability as Verno.'

Jerry Verno (centre)
and Eric Pavitt (right) in
My Friend the King

1931

Stranglehold

Director	Henry Edwards
Leading players	Isobel Elsom
	Garry Marsh
	Derrick de Marney
	Allan Jeayes
Screenwriter	[Henry Edwards?]
	(from a story by Hugh
	G. Esse)
Cinematographer	Walter Blakeley
Producers	Henry Edwards,
	E. G. Norman
Production company	Warner Bros First
	National
Distributor	Warner Bros
Running time	66 mins

Allan Jeayes, Garry
Marsh and Isobel Elsom
in *Stranglehold*

Stranglehold was the first film produced by Warner Bros First National following its lease of Teddington Studios, where it was to make over a hundred productions by the end of the decade.

This was a revenge drama in which a half-caste (Allan Jeayes) gains belated revenge on the Englishman (Garry Marsh) who betrayed his sister. The Englishman has gained a wife, a son and a luxurious Thamesside house, but his prosperity is undermined by the half-caste, who is now a neighbouring doctor specialising in tropical diseases. The doctor scratches the son with a poison and offers to provide an antidote only if the man's wife will go off with him . . .

According to *The Bioscope*, 'the conclusion is sudden and unconvincing, though before it comes there is much to interest and amuse. . . . Though this story is rather drab and unfolded on melodramatic lines, it is noteworthy for some humorous character studies, is prettily staged and well photographed.'

Henry Edwards had been a leading star and director of the silent period and his *Lily of the Alley* (1923) is featured earlier in this book.

1931

The Rasp

Director	Michael Powell
Leading players	Claude Horton
	Phyllis Loring
	C. M. Hallard
Screenwriter	Philip MacDonald (from
	his story)
Cinematographer	Geoffrey Faithfull
Art director	Frank Wells
Producer	Jerry Jackson
Production company	Film Engineering
Distributor	Fox
Running time	44 mins

Pleased with the way that his story *Rynox* had been handled by Powell, thriller writer Philip MacDonald continued the association on *The Rasp*. In this featurette a cabinet minister is killed with a rasp at his country home. MacDonald's sleuth of a journalist Anthony Gethryn tricks the killer into a confession, providing his newspaper with a scoop.

'Just another murder mystery,' declared *The Bioscope*, 'and while there is a certain amount of mystery as to the perpetrator of the deed, the events which lead up to the solution and the arrest of the culprit are such as to convince only the more easily interested patron.' The reviewer was offended by the film's customary portrayal of Scotland Yard as dimwitted and demanded to know when this 'unjustifiable slur' on the British police would cease.

Kine Weekly commented: 'In tackling a murder mystery drama, in which a newspaperman is involved, Michael Powell, the director, has butted in on America's favourite theme, and this effort, although moderately good, suffers in comparison. However, the atmosphere is refreshingly English, and there remains sufficient to entertain the unsophisticated.'

The Rasp

Four scene stills from
The Rasp

The Star Reporter

Director	Michael Powell
Leading players	Harold French
	Isla Bevan
	Garry Marsh
Screenwriters	Ralph Smart,
	Philip MacDonald (from
	a story by Philip
	MacDonald)
Cinematographer	Geoffrey Faithfull
Art director	Frank Wells
Producer	Jerry Jackson
Production company	Film Engineering
Distributor	Fox
Running time	44 mins

Advertisement for
The Star Reporter

Page 40: Isla Bevan
and Harold French in
The Star Reporter

Another crime drama from a Philip MacDonald story, in which a newspaper journalist (Harold French) works as chauffeur to an attractive blonde society woman (Isla Bevan, in her screen debut) in order to provide himself with material for a feature article. He witnesses an elaborate smash-and-grab raid in Bond Street in which a world-famous diamond owned by the woman's father is stolen. He follows the thieves to their den and recovers the jewel after a roof-top struggle which ends with the villain plunging to his death.

Powell hired a hand-held camera for £8 and personally shot footage of the *Queen Mary* docking at Southampton to cut into the scene of the girl's father returning from America, which made the film look rather more lavishly budgeted than it actually was.

The Star Reporter received some exceptionally good reviews. From *Today's Cinema*: 'Exciting adaptation of story by Philip MacDonald dealing with jewel robbery, blackmail and murder. Charming romantic element links breathless sequence of thrilling incident. Cleverly directed on the lines of swift action, snappy dialogue and varied settings. General "thick-ear" atmosphere with admirably staged smash-and-grab raid, cold-blooded murder, sinister plotting and startling fire-escape finale developed with strongly emphasised suspense values.'

More significantly, the film critic of the London *Evening News*, A. Jympson Harman, declared: 'At the end of a long and not very inspiring day of seeing new films, I saw a little picture *Star Reporter* which jolted my tired brain into renewed enthusiasm. *Star Reporter* packs into three-quarters of an hour as much story as most films that last an hour and a half, cost £30,000 and take six weeks to make. It is absolutely without trimmings and tells an exciting crook story with a smoothness

STAR REPORTER

A Thrilling Drama of
Blackmail, Robbery &
Romance
from the story by
PHILIP MACDONALD

With
HAROLD FRENCH
ISLA BEVAN
GARRY MARSH
Directed by
MICHAEL POWELL

FOX
PICTURE

of direction and a crispness of acting and cutting which would be a credit to the most ambitious picture.'

Michael Powell later recalled: '*Star Reporter . . .* was fun and I was not ashamed of it. Harold French was a real pro. He understood comedy timing and I learned from him every day. *Star Reporter* played as the bottom half of the bill with Frank Capra's *Platinum Blonde*. I felt really complimented when one of the critics wrote that *Star Reporter* scarcely had the polish of *Platinum Blonde*. My film cost £3,700, the Columbia film $600,000.'

Leading man Harold French later became a director himself – of *Quiet Weekend* (1946), *My Brother Jonathan* (1947) and many other features.

1931

Director	Walter Forde
Leading players	Arthur Wontner
	Gillian Lind
	Edmund Gwenn
	Gordon Harker
	Jane Welsh
	Cyril Raymond
Screenwriters	Bernard Merivale,
	Harry Fowler Mear,
	Brock Williams (from
	the 1931 play *Jack*
	O'Lantern by George
	Goodchild and James
	Dawson, based on the
	novel by George
	Goodchild)
Cinematographers	Sidney Blythe,
	William Luff
Art director	James Carter
Editor	Jack Harris
Producer	Julius Hagen
Production company	Twickenham Film
	Studios
Distributor	W & F
Running time	75 mins

Condemned to Death

This was the film version of a contemporary stage production, a bizarre story of hypnotic influence extending beyond the grave. Before being hanged, a murderer hypnotises the judge (Arthur Wontner) who sentenced him, ordering the judge to kill the people he holds most responsible for his conviction. To fulfil the task, the

Arthur Wontner,
Gordon Harker and
Edmund Gwenn in
Condemned to Death

judge assumes a dual personality, masquerading as a mysterious figure in order to hire two toughs (Edmund Gwenn and Gordon Harker) to carry out the actual killings.

The Bioscope: 'Lovers of the murder mystery will find plenty to enthuse over in the adaptation from the play *Jack O'Lantern*. The story is not altogether a convincing one, at least not to the sceptical, but the general excellence of the production mitigates against any qualms on this score.'

Picturegoer: 'The characterisations given by the exceedingly capable cast and the ingenuity with which Walter Forde has handled the fantastic theme, succeed in making wild improbabilities convincing. . . . There are plenty of thrills and although the identity of the killer is never much in doubt the clever detail work and character drawing compels interest throughout.'

Help Yourself

Director	John Y. Daumery
Leading players	Benita Hume
	Martin Walker
	Carol Coombe
	Kenneth Kove
Screenwriters	Roland Pertwee,
	John Hastings Turner
	(from the novel *Sinners All* by Jerome Kingston)
Cinematographer	Charles Van Enger
Executive producer	Irving Asher
Production company	Warner Bros First National
Distributor	Warner Bros
Running time	73 mins

In this comedy, Warner Bros First National's second production at Teddington, stage star Martin Walker played a man befuddled by drink who throws a Christmas party at the castle of his rich aunt while she is away and discovers that the guests include thieves after the ruby necklace in the safe. A small Cockney crook (Hay Petrie) goes after it with dynamite and an electric drill; a bogus Major (D. A. Clarke-Smith) tries the touch method; another villain (Clifford Heatherley) and his vamp assistant (Carol Coombe) use oxyacetylene; but the heroine (Benita Hume) beats them all by knowing the combination.

The Belgian director John (Jean) Y. Daumery had worked with Rex Ingram in Nice and in Hollywood, where he handled French-language versions of Warner Bros pictures like *The Crowd Roars* (1932). Warners reassigned him to Teddington, where he made *Help Yourself* in both English and French versions. The latter was called *Le Soir des Rois* and shot afterwards (rather than simultaneously) with Jacques Maury and Simone Marcuil as stars (and a brief appearance by Daumery himself). Daumery remained in Britain, making a dozen more pictures (few of which are known to survive) before his death in May 1934.

Benita Hume was a bright and busy star of British stage and screen until she moved to Hollywood and married Ronald Colman.

John Y. Daumery, front, in beret, directing *Help Yourself*. Behind, in beret, Charles Van Enger

Hay Petrie and Carol Coombe in *Help Yourself*

Lord Babs

Director	Walter Forde
Leading players	Bobby Howes
	Jean Colin
	Alfred Drayton
	Pat Paterson
Screenwriters	Clifford Grey,
	Angus MacPhail,
	(uncredited additional
	material)
	Sidney Gilliat (from the
	play by Keble Howard)
Lyrics	Clifford Grey
Cinematographer	Leslie Rowson
Art director	A. Vetchinsky
Editor	Ian Dalrymple
Producer	Michael Balcon
Production company	Gainsborough
Distributor	Ideal
Running time	65 mins

Edmund Gwenn
(bearded) and Bobby
Howes in *Lord Babs*

Walter Forde returned to comedy in this film, with stage star Bobby Howes as the incompetent ship's steward who inherits a title and a big allowance. To escape marrying the daughter (Pat Paterson) of a pork-pie merchant (Alfred Drayton), he pretends he has become imbecilic and acts like a baby.

According to *The Bioscope*: 'With Bobby Howes as an imbecile steward, a bugbear to all those on the vessel, the fun runs high, for between secret gloatings over the photograph of his fiancée, mixing rare drinks in which metal polish is the main ingredient, and creating a general air of discomfort, he manages to keep the laughter going. The story's strong point, however, is his masquerade as a babe, and though the situation has some possibilities, Walter Forde has carried it to inordinate lengths, which develops eventually to ordinary rushabout comedy.'

Kine Weekly remarked: 'Bobby Howes is a bright and engaging comedian and his antics as the baby are sure to command the laughs. . . . It is Alfred Drayton, however, as the cockney pork-pie king, who runs away with the honours. His character drawing is brilliant, and his personality dominates the show.'

The 20-year-old Pat Paterson was signed up to work for Fox in Hollywood in 1933, but she soon retired to marry Charles Boyer.

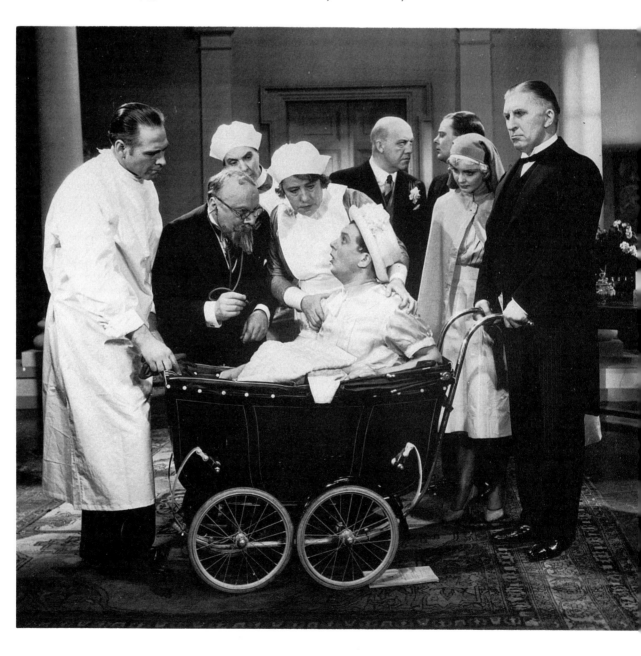

1932

C.O.D.

Director	Michael Powell
Leading players	Garry Marsh
	Hope Davey
	Arthur Stratton
	Roland Culver
	Peter Gawthorne
Screenwriter	Ralph Smart (from a story by Philip MacDonald)
Cinematographer	Geoffrey Faithfull
Art director	Frank Wells
Producer	Jerry Jackson
Production company	Westminster Films
Distributor	United Artists
Running time	66 mins

Garry Marsh (right) in
C.O.D

The first of the three pictures (all missing) made by Westminster Films, set up by Jackson and Powell as a partnership. It was another Philip MacDonald story, a murder mystery in which a man helps a girl dispose of her stepfather's corpse after he has been murdered in circumstances likely to incriminate her, only to find that the body has been returned to the scene of the crime. The man then poses as a doctor to clear the girl and expose the killer, who falls to his death in a fight with the hero.

Garry Marsh, the villain in *The Star Reporter*, here starred as the hero. In one of his earliest screen roles, Roland Culver – a droll and dapper figure in many leading British films of the 1940s and 1950s – was the murderer.

1932

His Lordship

Director	Michael Powell
Leading players	Jerry Verno
	Janet Megrew
	Ben Welden
	Peter Gawthorne
Screenwriter	Ralph Smart (from the novel *The Right Honourable* by Oliver Madox Heuffer)
Cinematographer	Geoffrey Faithfull
Art director	Frank Wells
Music and lyrics	V. C. Clinton-Baddeley, Eric Maschwitz
Producer	Jerry Jackson
Production company	Westminster Films
Distributor	United Artists
Running time	77 mins

Powell came a cropper with *His Lordship*, which was apparently far too sophisticated for audiences to accept. 'This effort, which starts off as musical comedy, drifts into burlesque, and then finishes up in a rich satirical vein, is neither flesh, fowl, or good red herring. It is very good in parts, but the good parts are outweighed by the bad, those which have no definite place in the entertainment,' said *Kine Weekly*. *Picturegoer* warned its readers: 'Jerry Verno, that clever and versatile British comedian, is very badly served with material in this queer mixture of musical comedy, burlesque and satire.'

Verno played the cockney plumber who is also a member of the peerage. He is persuaded by a couple of con men to become the fiancé of a tempestuous Russian film star anxious to marry into the aristocracy, thereby pleasing his mother but upsetting his regular girlfriend. One of the musical numbers featured a chorus of girl reporters, dressed in horn-rimmed glasses, tailored costumes and berets, writing in enormous notebooks, with enormous pencils, in unison to the music.

His Lordship was booed by audiences when it opened at the Dominion for a week in September 1932 as support to Ben Lyon in *By Whose Hand?*, alarming cinema owners who had booked the film. At their request, officers of the Cinematograph Exhibitors Association arranged a meeting with United Artists to see if they could be released from their contracts. The outcome went unreported but it seems unlikely that *His Lordship* was much seen. The title could be re-used without risk of confusing the public for a George Arliss picture four years later.

Jerry Verno and Ben
Welden in *His Lordship*

1932

Director	Michael Powell
Leading players	Rene Ray Talbot O'Farrell John Longden Ben Welden
Screenwriter	Ralph Smart (from the novel *Mops* by Oliver Sandys)
Cinematographer	Geoffrey Faithfull
Art director	Ian Campbell-Gray
Editor	Reginald Beck
Producer	Jerry Jackson
Production company	Westminster Films
Distributor	MGM
Running time	77 mins

Born Lucky

This film gave Rene Ray a singing role as Mops, a cockney music-hall performer who escapes the unwelcome attentions of a manager by becoming a hop-picker and then a domestic. She meets and falls for a tramp (John Longden) who is really a novelist searching for local colour. She becomes the star of a play he writes and marries him.

Kine Weekly described it as an 'ingenuous comedy', adding, 'the treatment shows some imagination, if the stars shine but dimly.' The hop-picking sequences were noted as being 'picturesque and original'.

Rene Ray and Talbot
O'Farrell in *Born Lucky*

1933

On Thin Ice

Director/screenwriter	Bernard Vorhaus
Leading players	Ursula Jeans
	Kenneth Law
	Viola Gault
	Dorothy Bartlam
Cinematographer	Eric Cross
Production company	Hall Mark
Distributor	Equity British
Running time	62 mins

On Thin Ice is one of the most obscure of missing British films. Its production seems to have gone unreported in the trade press and fan magazines. Its release date is not on record. No scene stills or publicity handouts appear to survive. It was a quota quickie for one of the least prestigious distributors and lacked any well-known players apart from Ursula Jeans. But it marks the first feature directed by Bernard Vorhaus (following some shorts for the *Camera Cocktales* series), made through his own company (Hall Mark) and apparently written and produced by him.

A society drama, the film centred on Ursula Jeans's Lady Violet. She becomes engaged, and a jealous rival arranges for a nightclub dancer to make love to her fiancé while he is drunk and then attempt to blackmail his father.

According to a publicity description preceding the trade show, 'The settings are spectacular and picturesque, and vary from scenes of noble mansions and beautiful sylvan scenery to the hectic gaieties of night clubs and the contrasting sombreness of high finance in the city.'

The *Kine Weekly* review was not favourable: 'So competent a stage actress as Ursula Jeans is ill-served by a production which does not add to the prestige of British pictures. The plot, which attempts a portrayal of Society life, is thin, while the treatment is not sufficient to win approval from any but an uncritical audience.' Yet a month later the same journal was full of praise for Vorhaus's second feature.

1933

Money for Speed

US title	*Daredevils of the Earth*
Director	Bernard Vorhaus
Leading players	Ida Lupino
	Cyril McLaglen
	John Loder
	Moore Marriott
	Marie Ault
Screenwriters	Vera Allinson,
	Lionel Hale,
	Monica Ewer (from a
	story by Bernard
	Vorhaus)
Cinematographer	Eric Cross
Editor	David Lean
Producer	Bernard Vorhaus
Production company	Hall Mark
Distributor	United Artists
Running time	73 mins

Bernard Vorhaus's second feature starred Cyril McLaglen and John Loder as rival speedway champions and Ida Lupino as the girl who pretends to fall in love with McLaglen, then rejects him, as part of a plot to ruin his performance. He takes to drink and ends up riding a 'Wall of Death' at a fairground, but a display of courage wins him the devotion of Lupino after all. Speedway sequences were filmed at Wembley.

'Here we have that rara avis, a successful British action drama, and its producers are to be congratulated on bringing to the screen the thrills of a popular British

Cyril McLaglen, Ida Lupino and John Loder in *Money for Speed*

Ida Lupino and Cyril McLaglen in *Money for Speed*

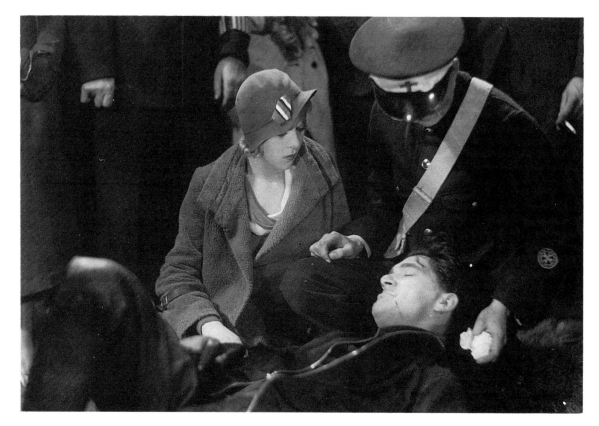

sport – speedway racing – and linking them with a straightforward but convincing story,' wrote *Picturegoer*.

Kine Weekly was equally enthusiastic: 'The characterisation is good, the atmosphere is authentic, and the hectic stunts deftly supply a hearty kick at even intervals which gives the picture slick momentum. One of the all too few successful British dramas.'

Money for Speed represents early work by David Lean, whose editing must have played some part in the film's impact, and the third screen appearance of the then sixteen-year-old Ida Lupino.

1933

Her Imaginary Lover

Director	George King
Leading players	Laura La Plante Percy Marmont Lady Tree Roland Culver
Screenwriter	Randall Faye (from the 1909 play *Green Stockings* by A. E. W. Mason)
Executive producer	Irving Asher
Production company	Warner Bros First National
Distributor	Warner Bros
Running time	66 mins

Picture Show described this film as: 'Delightful light comedy . . . of an heiress who invents a fiancé to protect herself from fortune hunters and finds herself surrounded by complications. Laura La Plante, in her first British picture, scores with her sparkling portrayal.'

Just turning thirty, American actress Laura La Plante had been a top star in silent pictures and was married to Irving Asher, production chief at Warner Bros First National's Teddington studios. She starred in four other films at the studio: *The Girl in Possession* (also missing) and *The Church Mouse* (both 1934); *The Man of the Moment* and *Widow's Might* (both 1935). Percy Marmont, a silent star who had returned from Hollywood in 1928, here played a Lord who happens to have the same name as the fictitious fiancé, comes to complain but falls for the heiress. Lady Tree played the girl's grandmother who helps in her ruse.

The source material was already owned by Warner Bros First National, having formed the basis of two earlier Hollywood films: *Slightly Used* (1927) with May McAvoy, and *Flirting Widow* (1930) with Dorothy Mackaill.

Her Imaginary Lover

Roland Culver, Lady Tree, Laura La Plante and unidentified performer in *Her Imaginary Lover*

1933

The Silver Spoon

Director	George King
Leading players	Ian Hunter
	Garry Marsh
	Binnie Barnes
	Cecil Parker
Screenwriter	Brock Williams
Cinematographer	Basil Emmott
Executive producer	Irving Asher
Production company	Warner Bros First National
Distributor	First National
Running time	65 mins

A simple comedy in which two gentlemen tramps (Ian Hunter, Garry Marsh), both victims of the Depression, confess to the murder of an aristocrat in order to protect his wife – a woman (Binnie Barnes) whom both men adore and who they think is responsible for the crime. The real killer is revealed in time to save them from the hangman.

Ian Hunter was under contract as part of the Teddington stock company at this time. He left for Hollywood in 1935 to play Theseus in *A Midsummer Night's Dream* and stayed at Warner Bros and (later) MGM for the next ten years.

Binnie Barnes with Garry Marsh and Ian Hunter in *The Silver Spoon*

High Finance

Director	George King
Leading players	Gibb McLaughlin
	Ida Lupino
	John Batten
	John H. Roberts
	Abraham Sofaer
Screenwriter	not known
Executive producer	Irving Asher
Production company	Warner Bros First National
Distributor	First National
Running time	67 mins

Advertisement for
High Finance
(misspelling
McLaughlin's name)

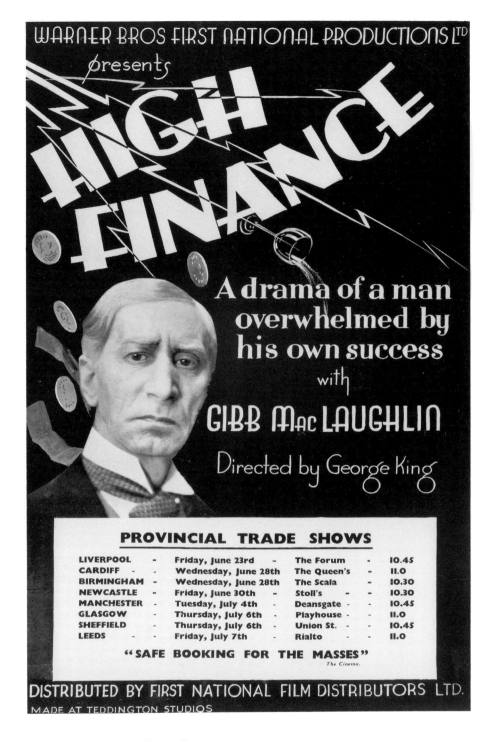

In this drama, a stubborn financier (Gibb McLaughlin) refuses permission for his ward (Ida Lupino) to marry. Ignoring advice, he becomes the chairman of a company which crashes and is sent to jail, where he becomes more human and understanding.

High Finance is principally of interest for an early performance by Ida Lupino, whose obvious talent had earned her a Hollywood contract by the time the film appeared.

No scene stills appear to have survived.

Director George King was known as 'King of the Quota Quickies' for his prodigious output of lesser features in the 1930s. He is best remembered for *Sweeney Todd, The Demon Barber of Fleet Street* (1935) and other horrific melodramas with Tod Slaughter.

1933

Director	George King
Leading players	Margot Grahame Harold French Carroll Gibbons and the Savoy Orpheans Clifford Heatherley O. B. Clarence
Screenwriter and lyricist	Paul England (from a story by W. Scott Darling)
Cinematographer	Basil Emmott
Dance director	Ralph Reader
Executive producer	Irving Asher
Production company	Warner Bros First National
Distributor	Warner Bros
Running time	74 mins

I Adore You

I Adore You

A musical romance out of the usual line of Teddington productions. The slight plot presented Margot Grahame as a film star who rejects the overtures of Harold French's wealthy young man (under her contract she is forbidden to marry). He won't take no for an answer and buys up the film company she works for. O. B. Clarence played an old actor who is mistaken for the young man (who has an appointment to view the studio) and receives a tour of the lot: this enables him (and the audience) to see numbers from a musical which is in production, as well as something of the inner workings of Warner Bros First National's Teddington studios. Margot Grahame and Georgie Harris performed and Carroll Gibbons and his Savoy Orpheans band were also featured.

Kine Weekly summed it up as 'A bright, unassuming song and dance show, a cheeky challenge to the type of entertainment at which the Americans are so adept, slight in story values, but bolstered up by spirited back-studio detail in which satire and showmanship play a prominent part.'

1934

Director/screenwriter	Monty Banks
Leading players	Laura La Plante Henry Kendall Claude Hulbert Monty Banks
Executive producer	Irving Asher
Production company	Warner Bros First National
Distributor	Warner Bros
Running time	72 mins

The Girl in Possession

The second Teddington production to star the wife of studio chief Irving Asher, this was more ambitious than the run of the studio's output, although La Plante's role was comparatively small.

Monty Banks (born Mario Bianchi in Italy in 1897) had been a top star of Hollywood comedy shorts who arrived in Britain in 1928. He demonstrated his flair for slapstick comedy when he directed George Formby in *No Limit* (1935) and *Keep Your Seats Please* (1936) and Gracie Fields (to whom he was married) in four of her best films: *Queen of Hearts* (1936), *We're Going to Be Rich* and *Keep Smiling* (both 1938) and *Shipyard Sally* (1939).

Banks not only wrote and directed *The Girl in Possession* but also appeared as an American confidence trickster in the opening sequences set in the United States, selling the stolen deeds to an English stately home to an unsophisticated American girl (La Plante). She arrives to take possession. The real owner (Henry Kendall) returns soon afterwards and she helps him sell the property to Americans, falling in love with him in the process. Claude Hulbert appeared as an aristocratic idiot, making such a strong impression that he was signed to an exclusive contract at Teddington with films written especially to suit his 'silly ass' screen image.

'Refreshing farcical comedy which runs a gauntlet of merry humour from New York to England and finds its artless but popular fun mainly in the individual efforts of Monty Banks and Claude Hulbert, both of whom cut lively capers. Situations are decorated with chestnuts, but such is the slickness of the direction and the good team work that they register well. The film makes a sprightly contribution to light entertainment. . . . The first half of the film has good American characterisation and allows Monty Banks to shine, while the second is essentially English, and finds its soothing humour in the asinine comicalities of Claude Hulbert' (*Kine Weekly*).

Henry Kendall and
Laura La Plante in *The
Girl in Possession*

Bernard Nedell
and Monty Banks in
The Girl in Possession

1934

The Blue Squadron

Director	George King
Leading players	Esmond Knight John Stuart Greta Hansen Cecil Parker
Screenwriter	Brock Williams (from the screenplay for the Italian film *L'Armata Azzurra*)
Executive producer	Irving Asher
Production companies	Warner Bros First National/Steffano Pittaluga
Distributor	First National
Running time	96 mins

The Blue Squadron was a new version of an Italian film, Ludovico Toeplitz's *L'Armata Azzurra*, which retained the original's spectacular flying sequences and replaced the leading players with British actors. John Stuart and Esmond Knight starred as friends and romantic rivals who are pilots in the celebrated Blue Squadron of the Italian Air Force. One of them saves the other's life while they are fighting the Communists. Becoming officers in the Blue Squadron, they fall out over the commanding officer's daughter (Greta Hansen). However, when one of them crashes in the Alps, it is the other's turn to save his life and their friendship is restored.

The film was recognised at the time as propaganda for Italy's fascist government, demonstrating its military might and preparedness. The British players were reportedly unconvincing as Italians, and *Kine Weekly* recognised the banality of the plot: 'The story itself is built up upon the familiar foundation of jealousy and misunderstanding, but the popular theme is nevertheless made the sturdy peg upon which to hang tremendous aerial thrills.'

Greta Hansen and
Esmond Knight (pair at
right) in *The Blue
Squadron*

1934   *No Escape*

Director	Ralph Ince
Leading players	Ian Hunter
	Binnie Barnes
	Ralph Ince
	Molly Lamont
Screenwriter	W. Scott Darling
Executive producer	Irving Asher
Production company	Warner Bros First National
Distributor	Warner Bros
Running time	71 mins

In this melodrama, Ian Hunter played a Malayan rubber planter accused of poisoning his partner. He is arrested on the false evidence of the dead man's wife (Binnie Barnes), who actually committed the murder. He escapes with a fellow prisoner (played by director Ralph Ince) and they stow away on a ship bound for England, on which the murderess is also travelling. The ship is quarantined when they reach port following an outbreak of bubonic plague, but the planter escapes and the police hunt for him is all the more intense because he may be carrying the disease.

Kine Weekly described it as 'a highly coloured melodrama of revenge and romance designed on lines that should appeal to the masses'.

This was the first film that Ralph Ince directed at the Teddington studios of Warner Bros First National. It should not be confused with a 1936 British film of the same title.

Ian Hunter, unidentified performer and Binnie Barnes in *No Escape*

1934   *The Office Wife*

A featurette with Cecil Parker as a financier who marries his secretary (Nora Swinburne), then falls prey to her successor (Dorothy Bouchier) on a business trip to Amsterdam. A divorce follows and the businessman marries the current secretary, but his ex-wife uses her wiles to win him back.

The Faith Baldwin story had been the basis of a 1930 box-office hit with Dorothy Mackaill, Lewis Stone and Natalie Moorhead. This modest re-make evoked reactions ranging from 'very naive and artless' (*Picturegoer*) to 'fair entertainment' (*Picture Show*).

The Office Wife

Director	George King
Leading players	Nora Swinburne Cecil Parker Dorothy [Chili] Bouchier
Screenwriter	Randall Faye (from the story by Faith Baldwin)
Executive producer	Irving Asher
Production company	Warner Bros First National
Distributor	Warner Bros
Running time	43 mins

Nora Swinburne with
portrait of Cecil Parker
in *The Office Wife*

1934

Bella Donna

Robert Hichens's romantic drama was one of many to deal with the exotic/erotic lure of the East for a white woman. In this British adaptation, Mary Ellis played a woman who visits Egypt with her engineer husband (John Stuart) and falls under the spell of Mahmoud Baroudi (Conrad Veidt), who persuades her to try to poison her husband.

The film was deemed old-fashioned and unconvincing, but G. A. Atkinson found some good points: 'Mary Ellis, whose allure is wistful and womanly . . . has a knack that amounts to genius for portraying the subtlest nuances of femininity. . . .

Bella Donna

Director	Robert Milton
Leading players	Conrad Veidt Mary Ellis Sir Cedric Hardwicke John Stuart
Screenwriter	H. Fowler Mear (from the 1909 novel by Robert Hichens and the 1911 play version by James Bernard Fagan)
Cinematographers	Sydney Blythe, William Luff
Art director	James Carter
Producer	Julius Hagen
Production company	Twickenham
Original distributor	Gaumont-British
Running time	91 mins

Conrad Veidt and Mary Ellis in *Bella Donna*

The outstanding quality of the film is the skill with which episode and setting have been moulded and blended to create a definite effect. The spectacle never subordinates the story, and the story leads up to spectacle in normal ways. There is no suggestion of a geographical lesson, which stories of this type are apt to become. The studio work reaches a very high standard, and Twickenham has every right to be proud of it.'

Bella Donna marked the first screen appearance in a sound film by stage singer and actress Mary Ellis, who later starred in *Glamorous Night* (1937). It was one of many films made in Britain by Conrad Veidt, who had emigrated from Germany following the rise of Hitler. The director was the Russian-born Robert Milton, who began his directing career in Hollywood, making the well-known *Outward Bound* (1930) and the Ann Harding film *Devotion* (1931). He directed two other films in Britain: *Strange Evidence* (1933) and *The Luck of a Sailor* (1934).

The story had been filmed under the same title by Famous Players in 1915, with Pauline Frederick, Thomas Holding and (as Baroudi) Julian L'Estrange, directed by Edwin S. Porter and Hugh Ford, and again in 1923 by George Fitzmaurice for Famous Players-Lasky, with Pola Negri, Conway Tearle (as Baroudi) and Conrad Nagel. A later 1946 version by International Pictures, called *Temptation*, was directed by Irving Pichel and starred Merle Oberon, George Brent and (as Baroudi) Charles Korvin.

1934

Father and Son

Director	Monty Banks
Leading players	Edmund Gwenn
	Esmond Knight
	James Finlayson
	Roland Culver
	Charles Carson
	Daphne Courtney
Screenwriter	Randall Faye (from the story 'Barber John's Boy' by Ben Ames Williams)
Executive producer	Irving Asher
Production company	Warner Bros First National
Distributor	Warner Bros
Running time	48 mins

Father and Son was a rare example of Monty Banks putting aside comedy to direct a drama. It was set in a village where a bank clerk (Esmond Knight) is disconcerted when his father (Edmund Gwenn) comes back from fourteen years in prison. The old man rescues a boy from drowning and takes a strong drink, only to be accused of drunkenness by his son before he can explain. Repentant on learning the truth, the son takes the blame for a theft that he thinks his father has committed, but the real culprit is eventually found.

This was one of many Teddington productions which adapted material owned by the Hollywood parent company. The same story had been used as an episode in *Man to Man* (1930), with Phillips Holmes and Grant Mitchell.

Esmond Knight and Daphne Courtney in *Father and Son*

1934

Blind Justice

Director	Bernard Vorhaus
Leading players	Eva Moore
	Frank Vosper
	John Stuart
	Geraldine Fitzgerald
	John Mills
	Roger Livesey
Screenwriter	Vera Allinson (from the 1932 play *Recipe for a Murder* by Arnold Ridley)
Cinematographer	Sydney Blythe
Producer	Julius Hagen
Production company	Real Art
Distributor	Universal
Running time	73 mins

Taken from a play by the author of *The Ghost Train*, this was a drama about a blackmailer (Frank Vosper) who tries to make a girl (Geraldine Fitzgerald) marry him by threatening to reveal to her ageing mother that her brother (John Mills) died a coward's death in the war. Her older brother (John Stuart) decides to kill the blackmailer, but his housekeeper (Eva Moore) 'accidentally' does the job for him and the girl is free to marry the man she loves (Roger Livesey).

The stars of tomorrow (Mills, seen in a flashback sequence; Fitzgerald, soon called to Hollywood; and Livesey) were apparently eclipsed by the work of a veteran: 'Eva Moore gives a clever portrayal . . . it is her flair for character drawing, born of vast stage experience, that causes the story's ingenious twists to register' (*Kine Weekly*).

Eva Moore in *Blind Justice*

1934

Director	Ralph Ince
Leading players	George Carney
	Eve Lister
	Robert Cochran
	Wally Patch
	Katie Johnson
Screenwriter	Michael Barringer (from an original story by Sam Mintz)
Cinematographer	Basil Emmott
Executive producer	Irving Asher
Production company	Warner Bros First National
Distributor	First National
Running time	56 mins

A Glimpse of Paradise

Apparently not even a scene still survives of this low-budget crime drama. George Carney starred as an ex-convict turned vagrant who locates his long-lost daughter (Eve Lister) even though her foster parents pretend she is dead. He is able to save her from a woman blackmailer without revealing his true identity. Wally Patch as the ex-con's vagrant chum and Margaret Yarde as the owner of a fish-and-chip shop seem to have contributed some amusing moments to what was described by *Picture Show* as 'fair entertainment'.

Eve Lister was given the leading female role immediately after she had impressed studio executives in a small part in *The Girl in the Crowd* (which was released after *A Glimpse of Paradise* and is also a lost film). Katie Johnson (who achieved belated stardom in *The Ladykillers*) had one of her many earlier character roles in this picture. Ralph Ince later directed another missing drama about parental sacrifice, *Gaolbreak*.

1934

Director	Ralph Ince
Leading players	Carol Goodner
	Barry Clifton
	Reginald Purdell
	Gyles Isham
	Eve Gray
Screenwriter	not known
Executive producer	Irving Asher
Production company	Warner Bros First National
Distributor	First National
Running time	48 mins

Carole Goodner and Barry Clifton in *What's in a Name?*

What's in a Name?

In this comedy of theatrical life, an insurance clerk (Barry Clifton) writes an operetta and submits it to two producers under an adopted foreign name. When a temperamental musical comedy star from the Continent (Carol Goodner) wants to meet him, he can't be traced under his assumed name and is thought dead. To encourage her to star in the operetta, the impresarios hire a dim-witted tap dancer to masquerade as the author. In the end, the real author appears and romance blossoms between him and the foreign star, who proves to be really a girl from the provinces.

One of the two producers was played by George Zucco, later a prominent character actor in Hollywood. This would seem to be the first of actor-writer Reginald Purdell's many appearances in Warner Teddington pictures.

1934

Director	Michael Powell
Leading players	Barry Clifton
	Patricia Hilliard
	Googie Withers
	Harold French
Screenwriter	Brock Williams
Cinematographer	Basil Emmott
Editor	Bert Bates
Producer	Irving Asher
Production company	Warner Bros First National
Original distributor	First National
Length	52 mins

The Girl in the Crowd

Googie Withers (left),
Patric Knowles (in
apron etc.) and Barry
Clifton (right) in *The
Girl in the Crowd*

A comedy. When a bookseller (Barry Clifton) marries a college student (Patricia Hilliard), she advises his best friend (Harold French), whom she has never met, that he should follow the first 'girl from the crowd' who attracts him if he wants to find a wife. By chance, he selects the very woman who gave him the idea and ends up in court for insulting behaviour.

Kine Weekly found it 'mildly amusing'. According to Powell (quoted in *Powell, Pressburger and Others*, BFI, 1978): 'It was a complete failure, nobody ever saw it. This was something somebody got out of a drawer and Irving Asher said, "For God's sake, shoot this." It was Googie Withers' first chance.'

Withers made another film that year for Powell, *The Love Test*, which survives. Barry Clifton was a Teddington contract player who didn't catch on. In the supporting cast was a Teddington discovery, Patric Knowles, soon to star in Powell's *The Brown Wallet*.

1935

Director	Ralph Ince
Leading players	Eve Gray
	Errol Flynn
	Paul Graetz
Screenwriter	Michael Barringer (from a story by Tom Van Dycke)
Cinematographer	Basil Emmott
Art director	G. H. Ward
Production company	Warner Bros First National
Distributor	First National
Running time	70 mins

Murder at Monte Carlo

A murder mystery of particular interest since it contained Errol Flynn's first proper screen acting appearance, in the leading role of a newspaper reporter investigating a new system for winning at roulette.

Previously the Tasmanian-born Flynn had appeared briefly in an obscure Australian production, *In the Wake of the Bounty*. He moved to Britain and worked in rep before presenting himself to Irving Asher, head of Warner Bros' Teddington studios. Asher signed him to a seven-year contract in October 1934 and gave him the lead in *Murder at Monte Carlo*. Warner executives in Hollywood were so impressed with his looks and personality in this film that he was summoned to Hollywood early in 1935, where, after two bit parts, he starred in *Captain Blood*.

Though Flynn was remembered by writer-director Delmer Daves as being 'self-conscious' in *Murder at Monte Carlo*, and more than one reviewer commented that character actor Paul Graetz stole the picture with his performance as the inventor of the roulette system, *Film Weekly* observed that Flynn and leading lady Eve Gray 'act quite charmingly together', while *Picture Show* declared that Errol Flynn 'gives a convincing performance' and *Kine Weekly* reported that 'the film is definitely a cut above the usual quota product. . . . Errol Flynn contributes a high pressure portrayal.'

Errol Flynn (left), Eve Gray, Peter Gawthorne, Paul Graetz as the corpse and Molly Lamont in *Murder at Monte Carlo*

1935

The Price of a Song

Director	Michael Powell
Leading players	Campbell Gullan Marjorie Corbett Gerald Fielding Eric Maturin
Screenwriter	Michael Barringer (from a story by Anthony Gittens)
Cinematographer	Jimmy Wilson
Producer	Michael Powell
Distributor	Fox
Running time	67 mins

Crime drama in which a bookmaker's clerk (Campbell Gullan) forces his step-daughter (Marjorie Corbett) to marry a caddish songwriter (Eric Maturin) for his money. She decides to divorce him to marry a newspaper reporter (Gerald Fielding) and her stepfather plots the perfect crime, the murder of the songwriter, hoping that she will inherit his money. Inevitably, he makes one disastrous slip . . .

Campbell Gullan was a prominent performer in silent films, including *Milestones* (1916) and *Lily of the Alley* (1923), both featured earlier in this book. In 1930 he directed *Caste* from a Michael Powell script.

Eric Maturin, Marjorie Corbett and Campbell Gullan in *The Price of a Song*

1935

Mr What's His Name?

Director	Ralph Ince
Leading players	Seymour Hicks Olive Blakeney Enid Stamp-Taylor Martita Hunt
Screenwriters	Tom Geraghty, Frank Launder (from the play by Seymour Hicks, an adaptation of a French play by Yves Mirande and André Mouëzy-Eon)
Cinematographer	Basil Emmott
Art director	Peter Proud
Executive producer	Irving Asher
Production company	Warner Bros First National
Distributor	First National
Running time	67 mins

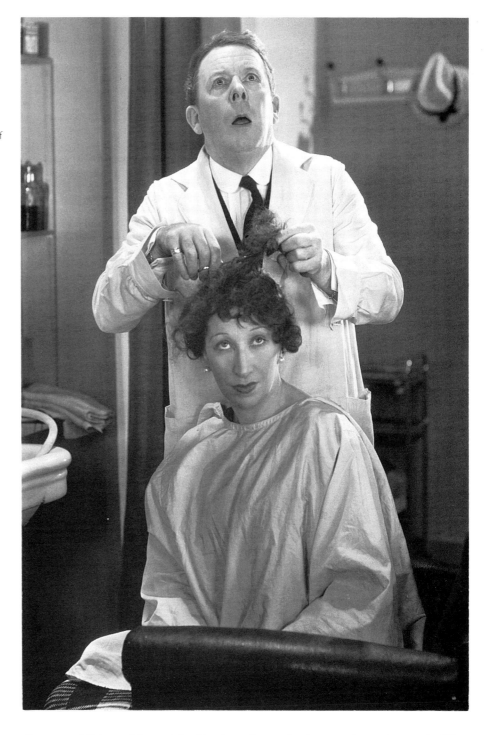

Seymour Hicks and
Martita Hunt in *Mr
What's His Name*

Seymour Hicks, celebrated for his charming and witty starring roles on the West End stage, had recently been confined to uncharacteristic film parts when Warner Bros gave him a chance to show off his comedy talent by starring in a screen version of his 1927 stage success about the adventures of an amnesiac. The play had been purchased long before by Warner Bros for filming in Hollywood as *The Matrimonial Bed* (1930), shown in Britain as *A Matrimonial Problem*, starring Frank Fay. (It was filmed again as *Kisses for Breakfast* with Dennis Morgan, released in 1941.)

In *Mr What's His Name* Hicks played a retired millionaire who has made a fortune in pickles. After a bump on the head in a train accident, he takes on a new identity as Monsieur Herbert Herbert, a beauty specialist, and marries his business partner (Olive Blakeney). A meeting with his first wife (Enid Stamp-Taylor) restores his memory, but she has since remarried and it needs another knock on the head to return him to a happier life with wife number two.

Kine Weekly commented: 'Snappy farcical comedy, the story of which approaches the loss of memory theme from a piquant angle. Seymour Hicks, who scored so brilliantly in the stage success from which it is adapted, repeats his clever performance, and it is to his consummate genius, versatility and eager buoyancy that the film owes much of its wit and sparkling humour.'

The Times declared: 'The idea is, of course, artificial and sometimes the humour is forced, but the high spirits, the indomitable gaiety, and, let it be added, the genuine hard work Mr Hicks puts into his acting carry the film along at a proper pace.'

1935

Director	Monty Banks
Leading players	Claude Hulbert Gregory Ratoff Jane Carr Nancy O'Neil
Screenwriter	Brock Williams (from the 1925 play *The Butter and Egg Man* by George S. Kaufman)
Cinematographer	Basil Emmott
Executive producer	Irving Asher
Production company	Warner Bros First National
Distributor	Warner Bros
Running time	70 mins

Hello Sweetheart

After starring in *So You Won't Talk*, Monty Banks returned behind the camera for this assignment. It was the third of six film versions of the 1925 Broadway hit play by George S. Kaufman (a flop in London) which told the story of how a country bumpkin is persuaded to invest in a Broadway production and outwits the smart producers at their own game.

In this version, Claude Hulbert portrayed the simple-minded poultry farmer who is conned into putting his inheritance into a film by a luscious star (Jane Carr) and her scheming producer (Gregory Ratoff). Hulbert is left holding an unfinished production, which he turns into a burlesque that scores a great success.

The other official versions of the story were *The Butter and Egg Man* (1928); *The Tenderfoot* (1932); *Dance, Charlie, Dance* (1937); *An Angel from Texas* (1940); and *Three Sailors and a Girl* (1953).

Claude Hulbert and Jane Carr in *Hello Sweetheart*

1935

Someday

Director	Michael Powell
Leading players	Esmond Knight Margaret Lockwood Henry Mollison Sunday Wilshin Raymond Lovell
Screenwriter	Brock Williams (from the novel *Young Nowheres* by I. A. R. Wylie)
Cinematographers	Basil Emmott, Monty Berman
Art director	Ian Campbell-Gray
Editor	Bert Bates
Producer	Irving Asher
Production company	Warner Bros First National
Distributor	Warner Bros
Running time	68 mins

Romantic drama (told in flashback from a magistrate's court) concerning a lift operator (Esmond Knight) in a block of flats who borrows a tenant's quarters to give his cleaner girlfriend (Margaret Lockwood) a surprise supper on her return from hospital. The tenant (Raymond Lovell) returns unexpectedly, a fight ensues, and the lift operator is charged with trespass and assault. His girlfriend's employer (Henry Mollison) generously comes to his rescue.

Kine Weekly described this as a 'slow, meandering romantic drama, a dilatory tale of life below stairs, reduced to entertainment of negligible quality by excessive footage. The theme deals with domestics and its suitability is confined mainly to picturegoers of that class.'

It was a re-make, relocated in a British setting, of the 1929 First National production *Young Nowheres*, which starred Richard Barthelmess and Marion Nixon under the direction of Frank Lloyd.

Margaret Lockwood, Esmond Knight and Henry Mollison in *Someday*

1935

Get Off My Foot

Director	William Beaudine
Leading players	Max Miller Jane Carr Chili Bouchier Norma Varden Reginald Purdell
Screenwriters	Frank Launder, Robert Edmunds (from the play *Money by Wire* by Edward A. Paulton)
Cinematographer	Basil Emmott
Art director	Peter Proud
Executive producer	Irving Asher
Production company	Warner Bros First National
Distributor	First National
Running time	82 mins

Max Miller (left), Norma Varden, unidentified, Reginald Purdell, three unidentified and Jane Carr (right) in *Get Off My Foot*

Top music-hall comedian Max Miller, 'The Cheeky Chappie', had played supporting roles before on screen but this was the first time he had starred in a film. He embroidered his role with his own dialogue and bits of business, the result, as he described it to a reporter in *Film Weekly*, being: 'In this picture I'm myself, to a certain extent, but, at the same time, it's something of a character part. I am a Smithfield porter. I have a row with a pal, and he falls in the river. I think he's drowned, get the wind up, and imagine the police are after me. I go on the tramp, get a job, chopping wood, and finish up as a butler.' In fact, he finishes up as a butler with an inheritance and his employers try to marry him off to their daughter while teaching him how to behave in high society. His true affections are reserved for the maid.

According to *Picturegoer*: 'All the good old gags and some new ones are incorporated in this robust broad comedy, which is designed to exploit the humour of Max Miller and will doubtless please his numerous following. There is rather more polish about this production than in most comedies of its type, but it is the slapstick fooling which gives it its mass appeal. . . . Max Miller carries the weight of the entertainment on his shoulders, and at times the load seems to be a bit too heavy; but the irresponsible comedian puts over his own type of material well.'

1935

Director	Ralph Ince
Leading players	Ellis Irving
	Wylie Watson
	Aileen Marson
Screenwriters	Paul Gangelin,
	Frank Launder,
	Michael Barringer (from
	the novel *Blackshirt* by
	Bruce Graeme)
Cinematographer	Basil Emmott
Art director	Peter Proud
Executive producer	Irving Asher
Production company	Warner Bros First
	National
Distributor	Warner Bros
Running time	67 mins

Black Mask

Known in production as *The Gentleman in Black*, this was a *Raffles*-type comedy-crime drama in which Ellis Irving played a gentleman crook who steals rich people's jewels and forces them to make charitable donations before returning their valuables. He falls in love with the niece of his latest victim, a newspaper magnate (Herbert Lomas). When the man is found murdered, he becomes the natural suspect and has to expose the real killer to clear himself. Wylie Watson appeared as the Cockney lag who lends him a hand.

Aileen Marson in *Black Mask*

1935

Dark World

Director	Bernard Vorhaus
Leading players	Tamara Desni
	Hugh Brooke
	Leon Quartermaine
	Olga Lindo
	Googie Withers
Screenwriter	Hugh Brooke (from a story by Leslie Landau and Selwyn Jepson)
Dance director	Hedley Briggs
Music	Charles Cowlrick
Production company/ distributor	Fox
Running time	73 mins

Tamara Desni and unidentified performer in *Dark World*

'The thing that interests me most about this production,' wrote *Picturegoer*'s studio correspondent, E. G. Cousins, 'is the fact that Bernard Vorhaus is directing it. He manages to get a slickness and a smoothness into most of his films that are reminiscent of Hollywood product. Very few of our directors achieve it.'

The film's writer, Hugh Brooke, played a leading role in the psychological drama as a successful songwriter who beats his older (adopted) brother (Leon Quartermaine) for the affections of dancer Birgitta (Tamara Desni). Insanely jealous, the older man plots to electrocute his rival but kills someone else by mistake. His next scheme also goes awry but, rather than waste its ingenuity, he uses it to bring about his own demise.

The theatrical setting enabled Tamara Desni to dance as well as act. *Kine Weekly* commented: 'Triangle drama, conventional in theme, but modern in interpretation and presentation. The treatment is a trifle high-falutin' at times, but the cast-iron fundamentals nevertheless gain adequate recognition and bring to the screen situations that are well charged with arresting suspense. The acting, entrusted to experienced stage and screen favourites, is up to standard and the technical qualities are first class.'

1936

The Brown Wallet

Director	Michael Powell
Leading players	Patric Knowles
	Nancy O'Neil
	Henry Caine
	Henrietta Watson
Screenwriter	Ian Dalrymple (from a story by Stacy Aumonier)
Cinematographer	Basil Emmott
Production company	Warner Bros First National
Distributor	First National
Running time	68 mins

This is one of his early works that Michael Powell remained enthusiastic about in his old age: 'It was a very ingenious little thriller – too ingenious. . . . It's funny, when a thriller's too ingenious it becomes a little picture; when it's simple it's got a chance of being big. This was a beautifully worked-out little thriller with a young actor who was coming on fast and who went to Hollywood, Patric Knowles.'

Knowles played a young publisher in severe financial difficulties who keeps a wallet full of banknotes that he finds in a taxi, only to be accused of having murdered his aunt and stolen the money from her safe.

Screenwriter Ian Dalrymple's talent was recognised and he was quickly engaged on major pictures, including *Storm in a Teacup* (1937), *South Riding*, *Pygmalion* and *The Citadel* (all 1938). He later became a leading British producer of such films as *The Wooden Horse* (1950).

Patric Knowles (left) and three unidentified performers in *The Brown Wallet*

1936

Gaolbreak

Director	Ralph Ince
Leading players	Ralph Ince
	Pat Fitzpatrick
	Basil Gill
	Raymond Lovell
Screenwriter	Michael Barringer
Cinematographer	Basil Emmott
Executive producer	Irving Asher
Production company	Warner Bros First National
Distributor	First National
Running time	64 mins

Ralph Ince directed and starred in this crime drama, filmed as *Bill and Son*. He played a convict who escapes from gaol because he is worried about the welfare of his young son, who is being looked after by crooks. With the help of a woman barge owner on the Thames estuary, he discovers that his child is being presented to a rich American couple as their son, kidnapped many years previously. When the father realises how well his boy will be looked after by the Americans, he decides not to interfere and returns to his gaol cell.

This imitation of a sentimental Wallace Beery picture (right down to a barge owner reminiscent of Marie Dressler in *Tugboat Annie*) certainly suited Ince's own roughneck performing style, and it apparently worked very well. *Kine Weekly* remarked: 'Popular sentiment is likely to be gripped by an unusual story of child kidnapping, the underworld, and a father's self-sacrifice for his boy.' And the *Monthly Film Bulletin* wrote: 'A drama of father love, not over-sentimentalised and made poignant by many human touches. . . . The child, Pat Fitzpatrick, is amazingly natural, passionately fond of his father, awkward and suspicious with others. Ralph Ince as Jim is a rough diamond with an understandable urge to risk anything for Mickie's sake and Elliot Mason, as Euphy, the barge owner, is a joy every time she opens her mouth. The settings are realistic. A film out of the usual run.'

The National Film Archive has only this one picture from the film in its stills collection, perhaps the sole remaining image anywhere.

Elliot Mason and Ralph Ince in *Gaolbreak*

1936

Director Michael Powell

Leading players Hugh Williams
Jane Baxter
Maurice Schwartz
Donald Calthrop

Screenwriters Ian Hay,
Sidney Courtenay
(from an adaptation by
Jack Byrd of the novel
*The Chase of the
Golden Plate* by Jacques
Futrelle)

Cinematographer Ernest Palmer

Producer Joe Rock

Production company Joe Rock Studios

Distributor MGM

Running time 79 mins

The Man Behind the Mask

Melodrama in which a girl (Jane Baxter) is abducted from a masked ball and her boyfriend (Hugh Williams) is accused of stealing a valuable shield from her father (Peter Gawthorne). The criminal proves to be a mad astronomer (Maurice Schwartz).

Michael Powell: 'They had a very poor script. I did my best to make it into a rather German type expressionistic thriller. It was very hard work indeed because we had no money.'

Kine Weekly: 'Sensational melodrama entirely unconvincing as to plot, but holding the attention by its extremely good acting and some clever touches of production which introduce the human note. Michael Powell has done everything possible to give plausibility to the tale; he provides a clear continuity, concentrates on facial expression and detail rather than background, and is responsible for many amusing touches. Melodramatic atmosphere is preserved throughout, with the usual humorous quips lightening the tension. The ending is disappointing, the ravings of the madman, whose one passion is possession of the shield, containing insufficient philosophy to interest. Dialogue, by Ian Hay, as might be expected, is entirely successful, especially in its lighter moments.' Ian Hay's other film work includes writing dialogue for Hitchcock's *The 39 Steps* (1935), *The Secret Agent* and *Sabotage* (both 1936).

Monthly Film Bulletin: 'The story is melodramatic and absurd but, technically, the film is excellent. Direction, photography, lighting, acting and sound are all

The Man Behind the Mask

good. The glimpses of family life . . . are extremely realistic, the country scenes are lovely and the final scenes in the crook's house are impressive when they might so easily have been merely ludicrous. All the acting is competent but Donald Calthrop as the chess-playing Dr Walpole and Kitty Kelly as his American secretary give the most polished performances. Martin [*sic*] Schwartz is good but his part being so usual is less difficult. But on the whole, the director is to be most congratulated for having made what must be termed a good film out of very unlikely material.'

The film had a significant outcome for Powell: he interested the producer, Joe Rock, in making what would be his first personal work, *The Edge of the World*, with which he bade farewell to the world of quota quickies.

Hugh Williams, Donald Calthrop, Ronald Ward, Peter Gawthorne, Maurice Schwartz and Moyna Fagan in *The Man Behind the Mask*

1936

Director	Paul L. Stein
Leading players	Jean Muir
	Gene Gerrard
	Hans Sonker
	Chili Bouchier
	Margaret Yarde
Screenwriter	Brock Williams
Cinematographer	Basil Emmott
Art director	Peter Proud
Editor	Leslie Norman
Executive producer	Irving Asher
Production company	Warner Bros First National
Distributor	Warner Bros
Running time	78 mins

Faithful

This film was the Warner Bros Teddington studio's first major plunge into the musical field and, to ensure a quality production, the leading exponent of the genre in Britain was hired to direct. Paul L. Stein had directed Richard Tauber's first two films in Britain, *Blossom Time* (1934) and *Heart's Desire* (1935), as well as the circus drama *Red Wagon* (1933). Austrian-born, he moved to Britain after making films in Germany and Hollywood and worked here for the rest of his career, directing such productions as *Poison Pen* (1939) and *Waltz Time* (1945) before his death in 1951.

On *Faithful*, he had as his leads Jean Muir, a Scottish-American actress who had just appeared in *A Midsummer Night's Dream* for Warner Bros in Hollywood; Hans Sonker [Söhnker], a popular German actor; and Gene Gerrard, a comedian playing his first 'straight' role.

The simple storyline dealt with a Viennese singer (Sonker) who has married an American (Muir) and with her support becomes the hit of London nightclubs. He is tempted by a dazzling socialite (Chili Bouchier) and neglects his wife, but an impresario (Gerrard) brings the couple back together again.

Hans Sonker and Gene
Gerrard in *Faithful*

1936

Director	Ralph Ince
Leading players	Henry Kendall
	Nancy O'Neil
	Joyce Kennedy
	Bernard Miles
	Grace Lane
	Ralph Roberts
Screenwriters	Frank Launder,
	Sidney Gilliat (from the
	novel *The Murders in*
	Praed Street by John
	Rhodes)
Cinematographer	Basil Emmott
Producer	Jerome J. Jackson
Production company	Warner Bros First
	National
Distributor	Warner Bros
Running time	64 mins

Twelve Good Men

A crime thriller in which an escaped convict seems to be killing off the members of the jury that convicted him, after sending them each a warning key. The survivors gather at the home of one juror, a famous actor (Henry Kendall), but the deaths continue. One of the jurors turns out to be the murderer.

This was the second collaboration of writers Launder and Gilliat, who had apparently bought the rights to John Rhodes's novel themselves and submitted an adaptation to Jerry Jackson, whereupon the producer started shooting it without making a deal with them. (See *Launder and Gilliat*, BFI, 1977.)

Kine Weekly's verdict: 'Murder mystery cleverly sustained, compounded with plenty of human interest and a love affair. Acting also and presentation, combined with the original plot and lively dialogue, entitle the picture to a good reception from the average patron.'

Nancy O'Neil, Henry
Kendall, Grace Lane
and Ralph Roberts in
Twelve Good Men

1936

Where's Sally?

Director	Arthur Woods
Leading players	Gene Gerrard
	Claude Hulbert
	Reginald Purdell
	Chili Bouchier
	Renee Gadd
	Violet Farebrother
	Athole Stewart
Screenwriters	Brock Williams,
	Frank Launder
Cinematographer	Basil Emmott
Art director	Peter Proud
Executive producer	Irving Asher
Production company	Warner Bros First
	National
Distributor	First National
Running time	71 mins

Filmed as *Three on a Honeymoon*, this comedy concerned a bride (Renee Gadd) who learns of her husband's past from a friend (Claude Hulbert) whose wife (Chili Bouchier) has just left him. She and her new husband (Gene Gerrard) have an acrimonious honeymoon, but all comes right in the end.

This was the first film that Arthur Woods made at Teddington, and according to Rachael Low (*Film Making in 1930s Britain*) it was 'much admired'. The *Monthly Film Bulletin* noted: 'There is a great deal of drinking and the humorous situations are frequently those in which the principal characters are intoxicated. Some of the dialogue is amusing, and it is made the most of by an efficient cast who work well together.'

Athole Stewart, Violet Farebrother and Gene Gerrard in *Where's Sally?*

1936

Fair Exchange

Director	Ralph Ince
Leading players	Patric Knowles
	Roscoe Ates
	Isla Bevan
	Raymond Lovell
Screenwriters	Brock Williams,
	Russell Redcraft
Cinematographer	Basil Emmott
Production company	Warner Bros First
	National
Distributor	Warner Bros
Running time	63 mins

In this comedy-drama, a famous criminologist stages a fake theft of a valuable picture with the intention of ridiculing his amateur detective son, who wants to follow in his father's footsteps. But the painting is then stolen in reality and the son successfully unmasks the culprit. 'An unpretentious but quite entertaining comedy-drama,' reported *Picturegoer*.

This was the last film Patric Knowles made at Teddington before sailing for Hollywood. As a result of his work in Britain, he had been given a long-term contract at Warner Bros' Burbank studios, where he appeared in *The Charge of the Light Brigade*, *The Adventures of Robin Hood* and many others. Roscoe Ates came over from Hollywood for *Fair Exchange* to bring his stuttering humour to the supporting role of Elmer Goodge, an over-age undergraduate still trying to pass his exams.

Patric Knowles and Roscoe Ates in *Fair Exchange*

1936

Gypsy Melody

Director	Edmond T. Gréville
Leading players	Lupe Velez
	Alfred Rode
	Jerry Verno
	Raymond Lovell
	Margaret Yarde
	Fred Duprez
Screenwriters	Irving Leroy,
	Dan Weldon (from the
	screenplay for the 1935
	French film *Juanita*, by
	René Pujol)
Cinematographer	Claude Friese-Greene
Songs	Bruce Sievier
Producers	Leon Hepner,
	Emil E. Reinert
Production company	British Artistic
Distributor	Wardour
Running time	77 mins

Made to showcase the talents of Alfred Rode and his tzigane (gypsy) orchestra, this Ruritanian musical comedy was the English version of a French film that Rode had produced and starred in the year before. The Mexican-born Lupe Velez came from Hollywood for her second British film (following *The Morals of Marcus*, 1935). However, its greatest potential interest now is as the first of the many films made in Britain by Edmond T. Gréville. It was Gréville who founded the producing company, British Artistic, in June 1935. *Gypsy Melody* was the only film made, and the company was wound up in 1937, still owing money to a financial group.

In *Gypsy Melody*, Rode played a captain of the guard who is jailed for a duelling incident, escapes, and joins a gypsy encampment where he plays the violin and wins the heart of a dancer (Lupe Velez). They achieve great success as performers and are touring Europe when their plane crashes in Rode's home country, where he is greeted as a celebrity and marries the dancer in a traditional Romany wedding.

Kine Weekly commented that 'Attention has been concentrated on the few big scenes, the minor ones indicating drastic economy. Editing has also been drastic, with scenes obviously omitted, leaving bad gaps. There are some nice touches of direction but the whole thing gives the impression of having been somewhat laboriously translated from a foreign language.'

The *Monthly Film Bulletin*'s reviewer found it a disappointing work: 'Except for one or two unusually beautiful exterior sequences and some interesting technical tricks the film shows little evidence of the work of the director of *Remous*'; and concluded: 'The music constitutes the film's major appeal and it is almost worth seeing the film just for the performance of Liszt's Second Hungarian Rhapsody, which is extremely well rendered by Rode and his orchestra, and excellently recorded.'

Variety was less critical: 'Charming country scenes, and general artistic backgrounds make this pleasing light entertainment; particularly for lovers of the vagabond type of music, it should be more than satisfying.'

Monti de Lyle, Lupe Velez and Alfred Rode in *Gypsy Melody*

1936

Educated Evans

Director	William Beaudine
Leading players	Max Miller Nancy O'Neil Albert Whelan Clarice Mayne
Screenwriters	Frank Launder, Robert Edmunds (from the novel by Edgar Wallace)
Cinematographer	Basil Emmott
Art director	Peter Proud
Production company	Warner Bros First National
Distributor	First National
Running time	86 mins

Of the eight films in which the fast-talking, brash music-hall comedian Max Miller starred for Warner Bros First National, *Educated Evans* was by far the most popular in Britain, both with the critics and the public, although Miller's appeal was never great in the north of the country. It was made by William Beaudine, a leading film-maker of the silent period who directed Mary Pickford's *Little Annie Rooney* (1925) and *Sparrows* (1926) and had worked with W. C. Fields on *The Old Fashioned Way* (1934) before coming to Britain. Besides three films with Max Miller, he directed several Will Hay comedies in Britain, including *Where There's a Will* and *Windbag the Sailor* (both 1936). His later Hollywood career saw him reduced to working with the Bowery Boys.

Reviewing *Educated Evans*, *Picturegoer* declared: 'Max Miller has rapidly developed into one of the best comedy bets on the British screen, and in this riotous farce, which is typically English in character, he is seen at his brightest and best. The production has the snap and sparkle which is too often lamentably missing in our home-made comedies; it also has a full share of wisecracks and perfectly timed gags. The great secret of its success is the rapidity with which the farcical situations follow one another; there is no let-up in the action.'

The *Monthly Film Bulletin* found Miller 'riotously funny as a racing tipster calling himself Educated Evans. He holds the field almost entirely on his own with a never-ending stream of apparently effortless wisecracks. His plausibility rescues him from all his escapades and the film ends with his winning a fortune by backing the wrong horse.'

Miller's biographer, John M. East, commented: 'The script was based upon Edgar Wallace's famous racehorse stories. The film told the tale of a fast-talking tipster, Educated Evans, who bluffed his way into the confidence of a couple of social climbers, who gave him the job of training their racehorse. The fun came from keeping up appearances while at the same time he forestalled crooks more unscrupulous than himself. With *Educated Evans*, and its sequel, *Thank Evans*, Max found his only tailor-made part in films. The cockney tipster, with his incorrigible cheerfulness, could not be put down.'

Thank Evans (see p. 86) is also missing.

Max Miller in *Educated Evans*

1936

Hail and Farewell

Director	Ralph Ince
Leading players	Claude Hulbert Reginald Purdell Joyce Kennedy Nicholas Hannen
Screenwriters	Reginald Purdell, John Dighton, Brock Williams (from a story by Paul Merzbach)
Cinematographer	Basil Emmott
Associate producer	Jerome J. Jackson
Executive producer	Irving Asher
Production company	Warner Bros First National
Distributor	First National
Running time	74 mins

Reginald Purdell and
Claude Hulbert in *Hail
and Farewell*

An episodic comedy-drama, dealing with the separate adventures of a colonel, a sergeant-major and two Tommies during six hours of shore leave from a troopship in Southampton. The colonel experiences tragedy; the sergeant-major is glad to be sailing again after a taste of home life; and the two Tommies have a hilarious time trying to be regular Romeos.

The *Monthly Film Bulletin* wrote: 'This is a very good film, well constructed, well photographed and well supplied with realistic and racy dialogue. The handling of the crowds and the excitement of arrival are extremely good and the fun is fresh and unstudied. The general acting level is very high, but Reginald Purdell who is also responsible for part of the dialogue, with Claude Hulbert as a foil, is the chief mirth raiser.'

Kine Weekly was equally complimentary: 'Rollicking comedy-drama of British Army life, combining thematic ingenuity with flawless character drawing and smart dialogue. The story contains many by-plots within its basic plot, and the cementing of the many into one complete and thoroughly entertaining whole is neatly and efficiently accomplished.'

1936

Irish for Luck

Director	Arthur Woods
Leading players	Athene Seyler Margaret Lockwood Patric Knowles Gibb McLaughlin
Screenwriters	Arthur Woods, Brock Williams (from the novel by L. A. G. Strong)
Cinematographer	Basil Emmott
Production company	Warner Bros First National
Running time	68 mins

Reputedly a comedy of exceptional warmth. In *Picturegoer*'s review, it was reported that 'Athene Seyler gives a remarkably good performance as an impecunious Irishwoman known locally as "the Duchess" whose imperious ways keep her creditors at bay and who finally puts a young couple on the road to fame as singers by storming Broadcasting House. Her "blarney" is very well put over, and her character is never too overdrawn for plausibility. As the young people she helps, Margaret Lockwood and Patric Knowles appear to advantage and put the songs over tunefully. There is a touch of theatricality about the proceedings, but the Irish atmosphere has been well caught and the twists in the plot are always amusing.'

Picture Show was equally complimentary. 'There is a refreshing charm about this Irish comedy. . . . Athene Seyler gives a delightful comedy performance as the

Duchess, and the supporting cast is headed by Margaret Lockwood and Patric Knowles, who are charming as the lovers. The Irish atmosphere is excellently conveyed, settings are well done, and the direction is deft.'

And the *Monthly Film Bulletin* concluded: 'This unpretentious film achieves much more than many more ambitious ones. The dialogue makes full use of Irish witticism. The acting is delightful and the atmosphere authentic. Gibb McLaughlin as the family retainer is superb.'

Margaret Lockwood and Patric Knowles in *Irish for Luck*

1936

Director Roy William Neill

Leading players Roland Young
Chili Bouchier
Hugh Williams
Frederick Burtwell

Screenwriters Brock Williams,
Terence Rattigan (from the novel *Tzigane* by Lady Eleanor Smith)

Production company Warner Bros First National

Distributor Warner Bros

Running time 78 mins

Gypsy

This was the first of the thirteen films which Roy William Neill directed for Warner Bros First National at Teddington, and also one of the first on which Terence Rattigan worked before he achieved success in the theatre. Rattigan signed a contract with studio chief Irving Asher and, while sitting around waiting for an assignment, offered to sell the rights to an unproduced play for £200. Asher told him it was no good – but it was eventually staged under the title *French Without Tears* and became a smash hit, later filmed by Paramount. In the autumn of 1935, Rattigan was given two weeks to create a script from Lady Eleanor Smith's novel *Tzigane*; his efforts were torn up and he was assigned to work with Brock Williams and learn scriptwriting from him.

In *Gypsy*, Chili Bouchier played a gypsy dancer from Hungary searching for the lion tamer (Hugh Williams) whom she loves. Roland Young was the kindly bachelor she marries when she thinks the lion tamer is dead.

Variety called it a 'splendid feature' and commented: 'Sounds conventional, but it's nothing of the sort. It is excellently acted by the three principals, well produced and so closely cut that much of the dialogue is lost in the laughter with the situations generally. Roland Young is the cultured, quick-thinking Britisher. Chili Bouchier gives so thorough an interpretation of the lively Romany that it is difficult to believe this English girl is not a product of the Continent. Frederick Burtwell plays one of those immaculate English butlers without making him a caricature.'

Chili Bouchier and
Roland Young in *Gypsy*

1937

US title	*I Married a Spy*
Director	Edmond T. Gréville
Leading players	Brigitte Horney
	Neil Hamilton
	Gyles Isham
	Raymond Lovell
Screenwriter	Basil Mason (from a novel by Paul de Sainte Colombe)
Cinematographer	Otto Heller
Technical adviser	Robert Rips
Music	Walter Goehr
Producer	Hugh Perceval
Production company	Phoenix
Distributor	ABFD
Running time	79 mins

Secret Lives

Newcomer Brigitte Horney played a German-born French spy who, at the end of the First World War, is convicted of being a traitor on forged evidence, while Neil Hamilton, a Hollywood star of the 1920s, appeared as a French officer who marries the spy as a matter of convenience and subsequently falls in love with her.

This was a deliberate attempt to make a different kind of war film. There were no scenes of actual warfare to distract audiences from the impact of war on the leading characters. Dialogue was cut to an absolute minimum: according to the publicity handout, 'no character speaks unless it is impossible to convey the scene pictorially . . . for more than half the picture there is no dialogue spoken.' This was intended to speed up the action, with scenes conveyed pictorially in a shorter time than would be taken by dialogue. As a result, the film required a musical score lasting forty-five minutes.

According to the *Kine Weekly* reviewer, director Edmond T. Gréville indulged in 'camera tricks'. The reviewer thought the film a 'rather highbrow espionage melodrama, the abstract story of which mirrors the mental rather than the physical hazards which are inevitably wrapped up in the lives of Secret Service agents. The story and much of the treatment are interesting, but there is a tendency to put camera tricks before excitement and suspense. . . . To be clever is one thing and to be coherent and concise is another, and it is because this espionage drama is more concerned with original camera angles than with the more essential operation of building up excitement and suspense that it has no powerful claim to consideration

Brigitte Horney in
Secret Lives

as a general booking proposition. It does, however, provide food for thought, satisfying entertainment for those who can discern drama in the suggested rather than the seen.'

1937

Director — Ralph Ince

Leading players — Claude Hulbert
Lesley Brook
Hal Walters

Screenwriters — Brock Williams,
Reginald Purdell,
John Dighton (from a
story by Stafford
Dickens)

Cinematographer — Basil Emmott

Executive producer — Irving Asher

Production company — Warner Bros First
National

Distributor — First National

Running time — 67 mins

The Vulture

A vehicle for the 'silly ass' humour of Claude Hulbert, this slapstick crime comedy cast him as Cedric Gull, an amateur detective who is taking a correspondence course in sleuthing. With the help of an old lag, Stiffy (Hal Walters), he investigates a diamond robbery and the abduction of the diamond merchant's young secretary (Lesley Brook) by Chinese gangsters. He chases the gangsters to Chinatown, where he disguises himself as a Chinaman to free her, recover the diamonds, and capture the mysterious master crook known as 'The Vulture'.

'Claude Hulbert fans should find this feature very much to their taste. The peculiar fecklessness of the star is well adapted to the super-inanity of the story, and the film, with its crazy humour and asinine "hero", goes all out for the well-known Hulbert effects – and gets them,' declared *Kine Weekly*.

The formula worked so well that a follow-up film, *The Viper* (also missing), was made in 1938 (see p. 85).

The Vulture marked the debut of Lesley Brook, a young Teddington discovery who was kept busy by the studio. Hal Walters also worked as a comic companion to Max Miller in *The Good Old Days* (see p. 91).

Unidentified performer, George Carr, Hal Walters and Claude Hulbert in *The Vulture*

1937

Director	Arthur Woods
Leading players	Keith Falkner
	Joyce Kirby
	Bruce Lister
	Glen Alyn
	Chili Bouchier
Screenwriters	not known (from a story by James Dyrenforth)
Music	Kenneth Leslie-Smith
Lyrics	James Dyrenforth
Dance director	Jack Donohue
Cinematographer	Basil Emmott
Executive producer	Irving Asher
Production company	Warner Bros First National
Distributor	Warner Bros
Running time	83 mins

Joyce Kirby, Bruce Lister, Keith Falkner and Chili Bouchier in *Mayfair Melody*

Mayfair Melody

Mayfair Melody was one of Warner Bros' more spectacular productions at Teddington, clearly aimed at first-feature status. It was a romantic musical comedy that introduced to the screen the highly popular radio and concert baritone Keith Falkner. This was the first of three films that Falkner made under contract to Warner Bros First National, all of them now missing (see also pp. 83 and 87). Here the well-spoken Falkner was improbably cast as a car mechanic whose singing attracts the attention of the boss's somewhat scatter-brained daughter, who arranges surreptitiously for an Italian maestro to train his voice. He goes on to win the lead in a musical comedy, and is briefly involved with a musical comedy star before returning to the arms of the girl who helped him.

With no previous acting experience, Falkner seemed stilted and self-conscious but reviewers praised his singing. Joyce Kirby portrayed the dithery, spoiled heroine, with Chili Bouchier as her rival. Given the participation of a Hollywood choreographer, Jack Donohue, the musical numbers reportedly looked impressive. *Kine Weekly* declared: 'Here we have a romantic comedy with tuneful song and effective dance ensembles that scores principally on its shy, disarming reticence. . . . The show lacks nothing in stagecraft, the musical ensembles that decorate the ending are artistically and ingeniously contrived, nor is bright repartee absent from the dialogue.'

1937

Side Street Angel

Director	Ralph Ince
Leading players	Hugh Williams
	Lesley Brook
	Henry Kendall
	Reginald Purdell
Screenwriter	not known
Cinematographer	Basil Emmott
Executive producer	Irving Asher
Production company	Warner Bros First National
Distributor	Warner Bros
Running time	64 mins

In this romantic comedy, a wealthy young man (Hugh Williams), disappointed in love, goes on a binge and ends up on the Embankment, where he is befriended by an old lag (Reginald Purdell) who thinks he is a gentleman cracksman. He is taken to a hostel for reformed crooks, where he is attracted to a girl who works there (Lesley Brook) and scrubs the floors to be near her. Complications ensue when he is grabbed by a gang who want him to open a particularly stubborn safe, but the girl comes to his rescue. Henry Kendall played the rich young man's superior valet.

Kine Weekly summed it up as an 'unpretentious romantic comedy drama of London life, presenting a spirited combination of clean sentiment, lusty rough stuff, and hearty slapstick'.

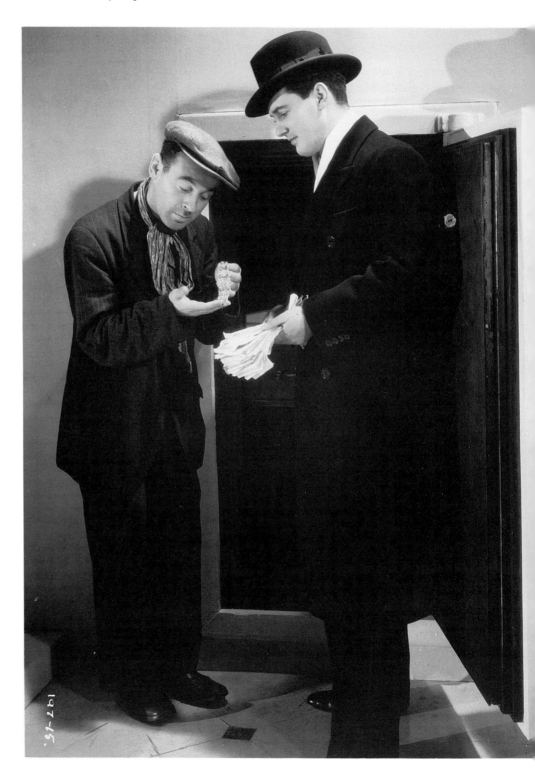

Reginald Purdell and
Hugh Williams
in *Side Street Angel*

1937

Director	Ralph Ince
Leading players	Claude Hulbert
	Henry Kendall
	Betty Lynne
	Violet Farebrother
	Sylvia Marriott
Screenwriter	Henry Kendall
Cinematographer	Basil Emmott
Executive producer	Irving Asher
Production company	Warner Bros First
	National
Distributor	First National
Running time	63 mins

It's Not Cricket

In this marital comedy, written by one of its stars, Henry Kendall, the French wife (Betty Lynne) of a selfish, cricket-mad husband (Kendall) decides to teach him a lesson. She persuades his best friend (Claude Hulbert) to accompany her to Paris, making it seem that they have eloped. The married couple are eventually reconciled and the friend finds a young lady of his own at a rained-off cricket match.

The *Monthly Film Bulletin* reported: 'Claude Hulbert conveys the Ralph Lynn attitude to life, and his absent-minded vacuousness provides plenty of laughs. He is well aided by the rest of the male cast, especially by Clifford Heatherley as an elderly bore whose Wisden is his Bible. . . . There are some vulgar innuendoes, and the flavour of naughtiness is not always in good taste. A humorous trifle.'

Claude Hulbert, Betty Lynne and Henry Kendall in *It's Not Cricket*

1937

Director	Arthur Woods
Leading players	Hugh Williams
	Glen Alyn
	Henry Mollison
	John Laurie
Screenwriters	Brock Williams,
	Tom Phipps (from an
	original story by John
	Drabble)
Cinematographer	Robert Lapresle
Executive producer	Irving Asher
Production company	Warner Bros First
	National
Distributor	First National
Running time	62 mins

The Windmill

A First World War espionage drama which presented Hugh Williams as an English lieutenant, billeted in a Belgian village, who falls in love with the adopted daughter (Glen Alyn) of the local inn proprietor. She is German by birth; a village tradesman (Henry Mollison), who is in reality an enemy agent, under threat of revealing her nationality to the authorities makes her carry messages to a windmill from where they are transmitted to the other side. The lieutenant falls for the girl, who sets the windmill on fire and is rescued in the nick of time.

The *Monthly Film Bulletin* remarked: 'The sets are realistic and the atmosphere of the misty Belgian flat country particularly vivid. The direction is smooth, and the acting good. Glen Alyn . . . gives an insouciant performance which well fits her part.' However, the *Kine Weekly* reviewer was somewhat critical of Alyn, and of Henry Mollison ('their accents are a little too ultra-refined for them to pass as characters of foreign extraction'), while *Picturegoer* asked: 'Why does Glen Alyn . . . speak in the unmistakable accents of the West End theatre?' Miss Alyn was a regular performer in Warner Bros productions at Teddington.

Glen Alyn and Hugh
Williams in
The Windmill

1937

The Compulsory Wife

Director	Arthur Woods
Leading players	Henry Kendall
	Joyce Kirby
	Margaret Yarde
	Robert Hale
Screenwriters	Reginald Purdell,
	John Dighton (from the
	novel by John Glyder)
Cinematographer	Robert Lapresle
Executive producer	Irving Asher
Production company	Warner Bros First
	National
Distributor	First National
Running time	57 mins

Margaret Yarde and
Henry Kendall in *The
Compulsory Wife*

Despite being the work of reliable Teddington regulars, this farce was savaged by the *Kine Weekly* and found weak and irritating by the *Monthly Film Bulletin*. The plot concerned a novelist (Henry Kendall) and a young woman (Joyce Kirby) who arrive independently at a country cottage to spend the weekend, only to find that their hosts have been delayed by a storm. The two decide to stay the night in separate rooms and are visited by a burglar who steals their clothes. In the ensuing investigation, they pretend to be husband and wife, which is not appreciated by the girl's fiancé.

Kine Weekly declared that the film 'has obviously been made for quota purposes and has no pretensions to compete as entertainment with pictures made with a definite box-office appeal'; and under the heading 'Points of Appeal' concluded: 'Hardly any'.

1937

Transatlantic Trouble later retitled *Take It From Me*

Director	William Beaudine
Leading players	Max Miller Betty Lynne Buddy Baer Zillah Bateman Clem Lawrence James Stephenson
Screenwriters	J. O. C. Orton, John Meehan Jr
Cinematographer	Basil Emmott
Executive producer	Irving Asher
Production company	Warner Bros First National
Distributor	First National
Running time	78 mins

Betty Lynne and Max Miller in *Transatlantic Trouble*

Warners followed the huge success of *Educated Evans* with this Max Miller comedy in which the Cheeky Chappie portrayed a smart-aleck boxing manager called Albert Hall. The wealthy, lovelorn Lady Fairhaven takes a fancy to his fighter on a voyage from New York, while Miller teams up with a gold-digger in a scheme to win the ship's sweepstakes. The girl outwits him and takes off with his fighter, but they eventually end up together in Paris, sharing an interest in another boxer.

Kine Weekly observed: 'Film differs from the average British comedy, mainly in the fact that the characters and situations are sufficiently realistic to give point to the humour, while many of the gags have a precision of timing in the best Hollywood tradition. The laughs are never forced, but arise naturally out of the plot development. Much of the humour, too, has a quality of subtlety that will appeal to the intelligent picturegoer without being over the heads of the masses. Scenarists and director have moreover given the star a chance to do his stuff without impairing the characterisation and story values or suggesting a music hall comedian putting over his act.'

Buddy Baer was the younger brother of former heavyweight boxing champion of the world Max Baer. Both brothers had extensive screen careers.

The film opened on 22 October 1937 at the Empire, Leicester Square on a double bill with a new version of *Madame X*, but had to be replaced within a few days. There proved to be a real Lady Fairhaven who, through her solicitors, objected to her name being used for a silly and flirtatious screen character. Warner Bros issued a public apology and withdrew the film. Redubbing changed the name to 'Lady Foxham', and the film was relaunched with a new title, *Take It From Me*.

The Man Who Made Diamonds

Director	Ralph Ince
Leading players	Noel Madison
	James Stephenson
	Lesley Brook
	Wilfrid Lawson
	George Galleon
	Renee Gadd
	Philip Ray
Screenwriters	Michael Barringer, Anthony Hankey (from a story by Frank A. Richardson)
Cinematographer	Basil Emmott
Executive producer	Irving Asher
Production company	Warner Bros First National
Distributor	First National
Running time	73 mins

A professor who has invented a system of manufacturing diamonds is murdered by his assistant (Noel Madison). The professor's daughter (Lesley Brook), worried by his absence, arranges through her solicitor for a Scotland Yard detective (George Galleon) to investigate. Meanwhile the diamonds, indistinguishable from real ones, are flooding the market. The girl is almost murdered when she discovers the secret, but is rescued in the nick of time by the detective.

The film earned some of the best reviews ever given to a Teddington production. 'Sensational crime thriller turning on a fantastic but gripping theme,' said *Kine Weekly*. 'Conventional romance plays a very small part in the treatment, but the keenness with which excitement is cultivated more than compensates for this omission. The principal male players get down to their jobs with infectious enthusiasm, and in their good work, backed up by realistic staging, is reflected robust, serial-like entertainment of unquestionable mass appeal.'

And the *Monthly Film Bulletin* wrote: 'Straightforward and excellent thriller. . . . The settings are good, especially those in the laboratory showing the Professor and Joseph manufacturing the diamonds. There is some first-class acting by Lesley Brook as the Professor's daughter; Renee Gadd as the foolish but faithful friend provides some genuine comic relief, and Noel Madison as the ruthless villain of the piece grips one's attention from start to finish.'

This film reunited Noel Madison and director Ralph Ince, both of whom had played supporting roles in the celebrated 1931 gangster drama *Little Caesar*.

Unidentified performer, Noel Madison and James Stephenson in *The Man Who Made Diamonds*

1937

You Live and Learn

Director	Arthur Woods
Leading players	Glenda Farrell
	Claude Hulbert
	Glen Alyn
	James Stephenson
	John Carol
	Charlotte Leigh
Screenwriters	Brock Williams,
	Tom Phipps (from the
	story 'Have You Come
	for Me?' by Norma
	Patterson)
Cinematographer	Basil Emmott
Executive producer	Irving Asher
Production company	Warner Bros First
	National
Distributor	Warner Bros
Running time	81 mins

This Teddington comedy combined the talents of the brash, rapid-talking Hollywood comedienne Glenda Farrell with the silly-ass humour of Claude Hulbert. She is an American nightclub dancer stranded in Paris who marries an admirer, Hulbert's nitwitted Englishman, visiting France to collect an inheritance. This proves to be worthless and she discovers that she has become hitched to a poor farmer, a widower with three children. Trying to make the best of it, she encounters hostility from the local villagers but settles down happily in the end.

According to the *Monthly Film Bulletin*, 'the distinctive types of humour represented by Claude Hulbert and Glenda Farrell do not blend well and it is difficult to accept them as a married couple: his Oh-I-Say style becomes vague and meaningless while Glenda Farrell's wisecracks by contrast with it become strident and acrid.' However, *Kine Weekly* found it a 'rustic romantic comedy introducing an Anglo-American team with possibilities in Glenda Farrell and Claude Hulbert. The story is more ingenuous than piquant, but the humour has a homely native quality, and this is wisely recognised by the stars and experienced supporting players. . . . Glenda Farrell is slightly handicapped by the leisurely pace at which the comedy is played, but her experience nevertheless serves her in good stead. She gets enough out of the part of Mamie to drive the story's simple point home and, at the same time, evokes no little laughter. Claude Hulbert is even less generously furnished with opportunities . . . but he, too, finds support in his own resource.' They were not teamed again.

Glenda Farrell and Claude Hulbert in *You Live and Learn*

1937

Who Killed John Savage?

Maurice Elvey's career as a director stretched from 1913 to 1957, covering all kinds of films from the noted war drama *The Flag Lieutenant* (1926) to farces like *Is Your Honeymoon Really Necessary?* (1956). His career was at a low ebb when he came to Warner Bros First National in 1937 and made *Change for a Sovereign* and the thriller *Who Killed John Savage?*, from a Philip MacDonald novel previously filmed by Michael Powell (whose version – *Rynox*, 1932 – happily survives). *Who Killed John Savage?* was known in production as *The Lie Detector*. Its leading player, Nicholas Hannen, was a theatre star.

Kine Weekly was full of praise for the finished picture: 'Ingenious, cleverly written mystery melodrama, one that can be depended upon to keep the majority guessing. The provocative, exciting plot is backed up by first-rate acting and

Nicholas Hannen (left)
in *Who Killed John
Savage?*

Director	Maurice Elvey
Leading players	Nicholas Hannen
Barry Mackay
Edward Chapman
Kathleen Kelly
Henry Oscar
Screenwriter	Basil Dillon (from the
novel *Rynox* by Philip
MacDonald)
Cinematographer	Robert Lapresle
Art directors	Peter Proud,
Michael Relph
Editor	Leslie A. Norman
Executive producer	Irving Asher
Production company	Warner Bros First
National
Distributor	Warner Bros
Running time	69 mins

resourceful direction, and flavoured by appealing romance. Just as the successful thriller of fiction compels the reader to keep his nose glued to every page, so will this, his kinematic counterpart, keep the average patron continually on tenterhooks.'

And *Picture Show* concurred: 'This entertaining melodrama may be relied on to keep you guessing. It deals with the murder of the head of a firm of chemical manufacturers, who is known to be short of capital. On his death, the insurance money puts the firm on its legs again – and then comes the surprise, for one of the men in the firm suspects that there is no such person as the mysterious man who is supposed to have killed Savage. It is neatly worked out and well acted.'

1938

Director	Arthur Woods
Leading players	Hugh Williams
Chili Bouchier
Garry Marsh
Reginald Purdell
James Stephenson
Screenwriters	Brock Williams,
Basil Dillon (from the
novel *From What Dark
Stairway* by Mignon G.
Eberhardt)
Cinematographer	Robert Lapresle
Producer	Irving Asher
Production company	Warner Bros First
National
Distributor	Warner Bros
Running time	73 mins

The Dark Stairway

Mignon G. Eberhardt's novel had already been turned into a 'B' mystery by Warner Bros in Hollywood – *The Murder of Dr Harrigan* (1936), with Ricardo Cortez and Mary Astor.

The most favourable review of this Anglicised version came from the *Monthly Film Bulletin*: 'Gripping story of murder in a hospital. Cresswell, founder of the Cresswell Institute, is injured in a motor smash and insists on a new anaesthetic being tried on him for the necessary operation. This anaesthetic and its formula is a source of deep jealousy on the part of several of the staff who wanted the sole glory of its discovery. Dr Mortimer, who is to perform the operation, is found stabbed in a lift and Cresswell is not in the Institute. Scotland Yard is called in and suspicion falls on Sister Betty Trimmer, which makes Dr Thurlow, house surgeon and lover, work frantically to set her free. The setting is authentic, the plot well contrived and fast moving and the acting extremely good. Chili Bouchier and Hugh Williams act realistically and James Stephenson makes an excellent inspector. The dialogue is crisp and natural and comedy, drama and suspense are all good of their kind.'

Other reviewers praised particularly Reginald Purdell as an inebriated patient, which contributed light relief to the story, while James Stephenson so impressed the Warner high command with his work in this and other Teddington productions that he went to Hollywood in 1938, where he had a busy career – most notably playing Bette Davis's lawyer in *The Letter* (1940) – before his death in 1941.

James Stephenson
(centre), Chili Bouchier
and Hugh Williams in
The Dark Stairway

1938

The Singing Cop

Director	Arthur Woods
Leading players	Keith Falkner
	Marta Labarr
	Chili Bouchier
	Ivy St Helier
	Glen Alyn
Screenwriters	Brock Williams,
	Tom Phipps (from a
	story by James
	Dyrenforth and
	Kenneth Leslie-Smith)
Cinematographer	Basil Emmott
Music	Kenneth Leslie-Smith
Lyricists	James Dyrenforth,
	Kenneth Leslie-Smith
Music director	Benjamin Frankel
Supervisor of operatic scenes	Percy Heming
Dance director	Jack Donohue
Art director	Peter Proud
Editor	A. Bates
Executive producer	Irving Asher
Production company	Warner Bros First National
Distributor	Warner Bros
Running time	78 mins

One of Warners's more ambitious projects at Teddington, this mix of grand opera and spy melodrama (filmed under the title *Music and Mystery*) starred Keith Falkner as the police recruit whose singing abilities earn him a special assignment – joining an opera company to watch Marta Labarr's prima donna, suspected of espionage. Falkner was a well-known baritone who had previously starred under Arthur Woods's direction in *Mayfair Melody*. Chili Bouchier played the socialite daughter of the opera company's principal sponsor, competing with the prima donna for the affections of the undercover cop.

By general consent, Keith Falkner sang better than he acted, but the plot was insignificant compared to the elaborate musical interludes, which were made with the co-operation of the Royal Opera House, Covent Garden. Its producer, Percy Heming, worked with Woods on sequences from the Third Act of *Faust*, which featured Covent Garden's chorus and costumes and Falkner singing the role of Mephistopheles.

Arthur Woods provided 'some deft directorial touches' (*Kine Weekly*), but the film's main appeal was to music lovers.

Unidentified performer
and Keith Falkner in *The
Singing Cop*

1938

Quiet, Please

Director	Roy William Neill
Leading players	Reginald Purdell
	Lesley Brook
	Julien Mitchell
	Wally Patch
	Bruce Lister
Screenwriters	Reginal Purdell,
	Anthony Hankey
Cinematographer	Basil Emmott
Executive producer	Irving Asher
Production company	Warner Bros First
	National
Distributor	First National
Running time	68 mins

Reginald Purdell wrote himself a choice part in this crime comedy as a busker paid to masquerade as a neurotic patient in a convalescent home. Discovering that he has been an unwitting accomplice of jewel thieves, he sets out with a fellow busker to clear the maid wrongly accused of theft. By using various disguises, they catch the thieves and return the jewels.

'Mainly a triumph for Reginald Purdell, who as street performer, nervous wreck, comic solicitor and housemaid puts over a rattling good performance,' reported *Kine Weekly*. 'Wally Patch is also in his element as, first, an old lady from Lancashire, and then as a "specialist" from Vienna. Realistic scenes outside a theatre, inside a pub, and in the apartments and corridors of a nursing home give an air of veracity to the various locations. The resources of inspired direction give out towards the end, but on the whole it remains a good job of work.'

Wally Patch, Reginald Purdell and Franklyn Kelsey in *Quiet, Please*

1938

Simply Terrific

Director	Roy William Neill
Leading players	Claude Hulbert
	Reginald Purdell
	Zoe Wynn
	Patricia Medina
	Aubrey Mallalieu
	Glen Alyn
Screenwriters	Basil Dillon,
	Anthony Hankey
Cinematographer	Robert Lapresle
Executive producer	Irving Asher
Production company	Warner Bros First
	National
Distributor	Warner Bros
Running time	72 mins

Claude Hulbert starred as an asinine playboy who has to become a success in business before his girlfriend's father will permit their engagement. Teaming up with a failed businessman, played by Reginald Purdell, Hulbert establishes a company called Socko Ltd, but they cannot decide what to sell until they stumble across a cure for hangovers and coax the recipe from the flower seller who owns it.

Contemporary reviewers did not think much of this Teddington production. Patricia Medina made her screen debut in the picture and made one other appearance in a Teddington film, *Double or Quits* (see p. 87), after which she developed her career elsewhere, including Hollywood.

Claude Hulbert, unidentified performer and Reginald Purdell in *Simply Terrific*

1938

The Viper

Director	Roy William Neill
Leading players	Claude Hulbert Betty Lynne Hal Walters Lesley Brook
Screenwriters	Reginal Purdell, John Dighton, J. O. C. Orton
Cinematographer	Robert Lapresle
Executive producer	Irving Asher
Production company	Warner Bros First National
Distributor	First National
Running time	75 mins

Betty Lynne and Claude
Hulbert in *The Viper*

A follow-up to *The Vulture*, presenting more slapstick adventures of Claude Hulbert's criminologist Cedric Gull and his assistant Stiffy, played by Hal Walters. This time, with Hulbert adopting various disguises, they help Stiffy's niece (Lesley Brook), who has been accused of theft, and a cabaret dancer (Betty Lynne) who is being hunted by a criminal called The Viper, on the run from Devil's Island. Both cases involve the diamond that the dancer is unwittingly carrying in the heel of her dancing slipper.

The Viper had a strong set of writers. J. O. C. Orton was one of the team responsible for the best Will Hay comedies; John Dighton, who had worked on Teddington's Max Miller pictures, would later make notable contributions to Ealing comedies like *Kind Hearts and Coronets*; and Reginald Purdell, better known for his acting work at Teddington (he plays a BBC announcer in *The Viper*), wrote many other comedies for Hulbert.

The film was not well received by the press. 'Considerable expense has apparently gone in the production of gadgets and stunts for this picture which would have been better devoted to a more humorous story and funnier dialogue. The film finishes in a riot of flour, paste, and bottle-throwing, which no doubt still has a fascination for the groundlings' (*Kine Weekly*).

1938 *Thank Evans*

Director	Roy William Neill
Leading players	Max Miller
	Hal Walters
	Polly Ward
	Albert Whelan
Screenwriter	Austin Melford (from a story by Edgar Wallace)
Cinematographer	Basil Emmott
Executive producer	Irving Asher
Production company	Warner Bros First National
Distributor	First National
Running time	78 mins

The sequel to the highly successful *Educated Evans* continued the adventures of Max Miller's incurably optimistic turf tipster whose tips never pay off. The plot concerned Evans's exposure of crooks at a noble lord's stable who are intent on preventing his horse from winning. Evans is also involved in trying to restore a watch stolen by his girlfriend's brother from an unscrupulous trainer, his efforts hindered by the stupidity of his tout, Nobby (Hal Walters).

But essentially the film's appeal (or drawback) lay in Max Miller himself, with his quick-fire patter and vulgar humour. The *Kine Weekly* reviewer declared: 'Max Miller is in rare form as Educated Evans: he not only looks the part, but happily augments Edgar Wallace's rich native vernacular with his own inimitable quips. . . . Here is a rare instance in which a sequel is every bit as good as the original. . . . All the gags are bright and, what is more, they follow through in slick chronological sequence to a highly amusing and thrilling climax.'

According to the *Monthly Film Bulletin*: 'This nonsensical story is very good fun of its kind. The direction is slick and resourceful, and the pace swift. Max Miller is in his element. He puts over a rapid stream of Cockney wisecracks, amusing patter and gags. His exuberance is unfailing and infectious. The crook melodrama of the stolen watch is entertaining burlesque, and the climax unadulterated slapstick.'

But to the reviewer in the London *Evening Standard*: '*Thank Evans* is bright in patches, but it is not as funny as the original picture.' The *News Chronicle*'s critic concluded: 'Invention flags now and then, but on the whole, in its broad, unsubtle way, *Thank Evans* supplies a good deal of uproarious fun.'

Max Miller (centre) and Robert Rendel (right) in *Thank Evans*

Hal Walters and Max Miller in *Thank Evans*

1938

Director	Roy William Neill
Leading players	Frank Fox Patricia Medina Hal Walters Ian Fleming
Screenwriter	Michael Barringer
Cinematographer	Basil Emmott
Executive producer	Irving Asher
Production company	Warner Bros First National
Distributor	Warner Bros
Running time	72 mins

Double or Quits

In this crime drama, Frank Fox played an English journalist who is often mistaken for a notorious American gangster. Boarding an ocean liner to interview a well-known philatelist, he is taken on the voyage. When the philatelist is murdered and the most precious stamp in his collection stolen, the journalist investigates and, after posing as the gangster he resembles, brings the criminals to book.

Kine Weekly noted: 'Gangster melodrama, made in England to the reliable and exciting American formula. Mistaken identity is the crux of the evergreen plot, and this is exploited with an eye to the main essentials. . . . There are times when the plot is a trifle involved, but in spite of its many strings, fundamentals are clearly established. Momentum is keen, surprise is frequent and the character drawing convincing. A British gangster melodrama, it is a first-rate copy of the real thing.'

Frank Fox also starred in two quota productions released by Fox in 1938, *Second Thoughts* and *The Last Barricade*.

No stills have been found for this production.

1938

Director	Arthur Woods
Leading players	Aino Bergo Keith Falkner Sharon Lynne Athole Stewart Bruce Lister
Screenwriter	Brock Williams (from a story by J. O. C. Orton and John Meehan Jr)
Music and lyrics	Kenneth Leslie-Smith, James Dyrenforth
Cinematographer	Basil Emmott
Executive producer	Irving Asher
Production company	Warner Bros First National
Distributor	Warner Bros
Running time	78 mins

Thistledown

This musical romance – the third teaming of baritone Keith Falkner and director Arthur Woods – was set in the cinema's idea of the Scottish Highlands, with the customary background of historic feuds between clans. Aino Bergo played a Viennese opera star who marries a Scottish laird and finds life on her husband's estate lonely and difficult. After her friendship with a member of a rival clan nearly rekindles an ancient feud, she goes off to resume her opera career. Years later, she buys the Scottish estate in the laird's absence, allowing him to return and find her with a son he had never known about.

The *Monthly Film Bulletin*'s reviewer commented: 'An unsophisticated story most attractively played. Aino Bergo . . . is a little stilted and self-conscious in her poses, but compensates for this by an outstanding voice and an attractive appearance. Keith Falkner . . . steals the picture. He has an engaging personality and an exquisite voice. Athole Stewart is also outstandingly good. An excellent film with a high standard of acting and photography as well as musical merit.'

Other publications (*Kine Weekly*, *Picturegoer*) found Falkner to be wooden again and were more impressed by Bergo, a foreign star new to British audiences.

Aino Bergo and Ian
Madden in *Thistledown*

1938

Director	Arthur Woods
Leading players	Elizabeth Allan Cyril Ritchard Edmond Breon Anthony Holles
Screenwriters	Paul Gangelin, Paul England (from a story by Edmond Deland)
Cinematographer	Basil Emmott
Executive producer	Jerome J. Jackson
Production company	Warner Bros First National
Distributor	First National
Running time	72 mins

Dangerous Medicine

This was the kind of film, the sophisticated murder mystery, at which director Arthur Woods really excelled. Elizabeth Allan plays a girl convicted of murder who is seriously injured while travelling from court in a police car, and Cyril Ritchard is the surgeon who makes medical history by removing a splinter of glass from her heart. Indignant at the prospect that his work will be in vain when she is hanged for murder, the surgeon facilitates her escape and helps her unmask the real killer. *Dangerous Medicine* was the first film made at Teddington under the regime of Jerome J. Jackson (former partner of Michael Powell in Film Engineering).

'This picture employs the *Thin Man* romantic technique down to the adoption of a dog, but its borrowed plumes do not conceal entirely the crazy extravagance of its treatment and by-play. Still, inconsequential fooling, vigorously applied, is, nevertheless, its saving grace and key to general appeal. By nailing humour to its improbabilities, the most conspicuous of which is its irresponsible dismissal of serious ethical fundamentals, first-rate light entertainment is established' (*Kine Weekly*).

'This improbable story is briskly told, and opens with a clever and ingeniously staged scene at the Old Bailey. Resourceful direction, crisp and pointed dialogue, pleasant comedy, and adequate suspense make this film thoroughly amusing entertainment. The team work of the cast is notably good' (*Monthly Film Bulletin*).

Elizabeth Allan in
Dangerous Medicine

Cyril Ritchard and
Elizabeth Allan in
Dangerous Medicine

What a Man!

Director	Edmond T. Gréville
Leading players	Sydney Howard
	Vera Pearce
	John Singer
	H. F. Maltby
	Ivor Barnard
	Jenny Laird
Screenwriter	Basil Mason (additional comedy by Jackie Marks)
Cinematographer	Ernest Palmer
Art director	Norman G. Arnold
Editor	Ray Pitt
Music	George Walter
Producer	Hugh Perceval
Production company	Phoenix
Distributor	British Lion
Running time	74 mins

Sydney Howard was a distinctive British comedian who progressed from variety and revue to stage and screen, making his film debut in *Splinters* (1929). He is perhaps best remembered for his work opposite Gracie Fields in *Shipyard Sally* (1939), where he was described by Jeffrey Richards as 'a revelation in his comic timing and comedic persona . . . a sort of English W. C. Fields, with his own weaving and swaying stance, expressive hands, fondness for the bottle, euphonious magniloquence and rhapsodically overdone courtship of middle-aged ladies'. Denis Gifford has summarised Howard as a 'unique comedian with stately style and strange gesticulations'. However, two contemporary reviewers of *What a Man!* referred to his 'bland humour'.

In this starring vehicle (completed by December 1937 but not trade shown until January 1939), Howard plays a professional photographer who is also a scout-master and secretary of a local 'slate club'. Vera Pearce appears as his ambitious wife who wants to see him elected to the town council. His various misadventures include photographing the local bigwigs at embarrassing moments and temporarily losing the slate club's funds, but he saves the local common from a builder's housing scheme and is ultimately elected mayor. The film required him to masquerade as a Chinese conjurer, a vacuum cleaner salesman and an old lady of 'doubtful gentleness and age'.

'Essentially a vehicle for Sydney Howard, it portrays the whimsicalities which brought him stage success, including his famous female impersonations. . . . A rollicking romp which should delight Howard fans but which is too reminiscent of a stage show to rate as a first-rate film' (*Monthly Film Bulletin*).

Sydney Howard and Vera Pearce in *What a Man!*

1939

A Gentleman's Gentleman

Director	Roy William Neill
Leading players	Eric Blore
	Marie Lohr
	Peter Coke
	Patricia Hilliard
	David Hutcheson
	David Burns
Screenwriters	Elizabeth Meehan, Austin Melford (from a play by Philip MacDonald)
Cinematographer	Basil Emmott
Executive producer	Jerome J. Jackson
Production company	Warner Bros First National
Distributor	Warner Bros
Running time	70 mins

Eric Blore in
A Gentleman's Gentleman

The London-born bald comedy actor Eric Blore, a Hollywood specialist in haughty, petulant valets and butlers, was particularly effective in the Astaire-Rogers musicals and in Preston Sturges's *The Lady Eve* and *Sullivan's Travels* (both 1941). He had a rare starring role in this film (his only appearance in a British talkie), playing a 'gentleman's gentleman' who prepares to blackmail a trio of young revellers over the apparent death of an elderly man at a New Year's ball, but settles instead for marriage to Marie Lohr's wealthy widow.

Part of the comedy was set at a winter resort in Switzerland, built on the Teddington sound stages. A topical touch was introduced by showing two of the characters leaving for the Alps on 'Ensign', the world's largest land-plane, which had just been delivered with much fanfare to Imperial Airways. The plane was taxied out on to the runway at Croydon Airport so that the actors could play a scene in front of it.

1939

The Good Old Days

Warners tried to widen Max Miller's appeal by putting him in a period outfit as Alexander the Greatest, manager of a troupe of travelling players in 1840 who end up in the stocks, pelted with squashy pears, for performing on unauthorised premises. After another attempt, they are heavily fined but saved when they collect the reward for returning the kidnapped son of an aristocrat.

Despite attempts, on top of the change of costume, to make him more sympathetic and have him speak more slowly for the benefit of more northerly cinemagoers, Max Miller was still his brash and exuberant self. As Paul Holt put it in the London *Evening News*: 'They dress him up in an old top hat, moth-collar coat, silver-knobbed cane, pretend he is a busker of 1839 vintage and ask us to

Director	Roy William Neill
Leading players	Max Miller
	Hal Walters
	Kathleen Gibson
	H. F. Maltby
	Martita Hunt
Screenwriters	Austin Melford, John Dighton (from a story by Ralph Smart)
Cinematographer	Basil Emmott
Executive producer	Jerome J. Jackson
Production company	Warner Bros First National
Distributor	First National
Running time	79 mins

believe them. A fat chance.' But, as *Variety*'s reviewer commented, 'Many will enjoy the picture in spite of him, and not because of him.' And, in the *Spectator*, Graham Greene wrote: 'I am inclined to avoid a Max Miller film, but *The Good Old Days* has one Regency sequence of a pie-eating contest in a public-house which almost makes it worth a visit. The sight of seconds massaging the huge stomachs of the contestants – the voice of the referee tolling out the score, "The Champion is starting his ninth pie, leading by four pies from the Camberwell Cannibal" – has a pleasant period grossness.'

Hal Walters and Max Miller in *The Good Old Days*

1939

Dr O'Dowd

Stage and variety star Shaun Glenville played the title role of an Irish doctor who enjoys a drink with his patients. Falsely accused by his son (Liam Gaffney) of being drunk and incapable while performing an emergency operation on his son's wife, he is struck off the register and retires to a remote district. Eventually an outbreak of diphtheria enables the doctor to restore his reputation and the son admits his error. The film marked the debut of the 14-year-old Peggy Cummins, 'a distinct discovery, and her future promises very well indeed' (*Picturegoer*). Another future star, Patricia Roc, provided the love interest with James Carney.

'This moving film is convincingly directed and ably acted. The kindly, humorous, impatient old Doctor is admirably portrayed by Shaun Glenville, Mary Merrell is delightful as his absent-minded but lovable sister, and Peggy Cummins is charming as his grand-daughter, Pat. The settings appear authentic and the Irish atmosphere is well captured' (*Monthly Film Bulletin*).

Director	Herbert Mason
Leading players	Shaun Glenville
	Peggy Cummins
	Mary Merrell
	Liam Gaffney
	Patricia Roc
	James Carney
Screenwriters	Austin Melford,
	Derek Twist (from a
	story by L. A. G. Strong)
Cinematographer	Basil Emmott
Executive producer	Sam Sax
Production company	Warner Bros First
	National
Distributor	Warner Bros
Running time	76 mins

Shaun Glenville and
Peggy Cummins in
Dr O'Dowd

1939

Confidential Lady

Director	Arthur Woods
Leading players	Ben Lyon
	Jane Baxter
	Athole Stewart
	Ronald Ward
	Jean Cadell
	Stewart Rome
Screenwriters	Brock Williams,
	Derek Twist
Cinematographer	Basil Emmott
Executive producer	Sam Sax
Production company	Warner Bros First
	National
Distributor	First National
Running time	74 mins

A romantic comedy drama about a jilted girl's attempts at revenge, *Confidential Lady* featured Ben Lyon as a misogynistic reporter who helps the woman (Jane Baxter) expose her ex-fiancé and the owner of his newspaper as the villains who ruined her father.

'This bright and frothy little story has a superabundance of dialogue, the element of surprise is lacking, and action is rather at a discount. But it is put over in exactly the right spirit. Ben Lyon makes a forceful, breezy and hard-boiled reporter. Jane Baxter is an attractive Jill, though she finds it difficult to be convincing as a gold-digger. The supporting cast is excellent, with an especially good performance from Jean Cadell as Jill's old nurse. Production values are good, with effective but unobtrusive backgrounds of luxurious flats and newspaper offices' (*Monthly Film Bulletin*).

Ben Lyon in
Confidential Lady

His Brother's Keeper

Director	Roy William Neill
Leading players	Clifford Evans
	Tamara Desni
	Peter Glenville
	Una O'Connor
	Reginald Purdell
Screenwriters	Roy William Neill,
	Austin Melford,
	Brock Williams
Cinematographer	Basil Emmott
Executive producer	Sam Sax
Production company	Warner Bros First
	National
Distributor	Warner Bros
Running time	70 mins

Olga, a gold-digging dancer-singer (Tamara Desni), comes between two brothers who have a music-hall act in which one, blindfolded, shoots an outline of bullet-holes around the other. Clifford Evans played the older brother, while future stage and screen director Peter Glenville was the younger. The stark outcome involves the woman's murder and the suicide of one of the brothers.

'It is not a pretty tale but it is deftly presented, with smart directorial touches, and packs a suspenseful climax' (*Daily Film Renter*).

'The story opens slowly and gradually achieves a rhythm of suspense. The photography is very sharp and clear, which helps to intensify the atmosphere of strain. The film is very well cast, especially Peter Glenville as the idealistic Hicky and Clifford Evans as the elder brother brusquely devoted to the younger. The minor characters are also well worked out, Una O'Connor as Olga's dresser, particularly, adding many touches to the detail of the story. The direction by Roy William Neill is excellent' (*Monthly Film Bulletin*).

Antoinette Lupino, Clifford Evans (blindfolded), Reginald Purdell and Peter Glenville in *His Brother's Keeper*

Murder Will Out

Director	Roy William Neill
Leading players	John Loder
	Jane Baxter
	Jack Hawkins
	Hartley Power
Screenwriters	Austin Melford,
	Brock Williams,
	Derek Twist (from a
	story by Roy William
	Neill)
Cinematographer	Basil Emmott
Producer	Roy William Neill
Production company	Warner Bros First
	National
Distributor	Warner Bros
Running time	65 mins

John Loder and Jane Baxter in *Murder Will Out*

Jack Hawkins plays a man who buys a valuable piece of jade during an air-raid in China for a collector friend in London (John Loder). Soon after delivering it, Hawkins is seemingly shot dead in the street and his body disappears. A friend and a crime expert also vanish and Loder's wife (Jane Baxter) receives a letter threatening his life. She delivers a large sum of money to the criminals, who prove to be none other than . . .

The *Daily Film Renter* advised its readers: 'Plot trifle complicated, liberally garnished with dialogue, but usual red herring clues introduced, and climax should baffle all but observant patrons.'

Besides *Murder Will Out*, Jane Baxter starred in three other films now missing: *Bed and Breakfast* (1930), *The Man Behind the Mask* (1936) and *Confidential Lady* (1939).

William (then 'Billy') Hartnell provided the comic relief as a cockney butler with a passion for canaries.

The Night Invader

Director	Herbert Mason
Leading players	Anne Crawford David Farrar Carl Jaffe Sybilla Binder Marius Goring
Screenwriters	Roland Pertwee, Brock Williams (from the adaptation by Edward Dryhurst of the novel *Rendezvous with Death* by John Bentley)
Cinematographer	Otto Heller
Production company/ distributor	Warner Bros
Running time	81 mins

Anne Crawford and
David Farrar in
The Night Invader

A typical wartime morale-booster, with David Farrar as a British secret agent parachuted into Holland and masquerading as an American journalist while seeking a secret document. Anne Crawford plays the sister of the document's owner.

'It has familiar undercover thrills of a popular order. It smacks of the old-time serial melodrama, but is well put over none the less' (*Picturegoer*).

'David Farrar rather steals this fast-moving and amusing film from Anne Crawford, while Carl Jaffe is excellent as a bombastic but blundering German colonel even if he slightly burlesques it. The finish is rather incredible, but the swift dialogue almost masks its weakness. A special word should be given to small-part actor George Carney who is superb as a train conductor' (*Monthly Film Bulletin*).

Only three stills from this film appear to have survived.

1943

Director	Brian Desmond Hurst
Leading players	Anne Crawford David Farrar Frederick Leister Mary Clare Richard Attenborough Niall MacGinnis David Hutcheson
Screenwriters	Brock Williams, (additional dialogue) Rodney Ackland (from a screenplay by Abem Finkel based on an original story by Mark Hellinger)
Cinematographer	Otto Heller
Production company/ distributor	Warner Bros
Running time	84 mins

The Hundred Pound Window

Frederick Leister,
Richard Attenborough,
Anne Crawford, David
Farrar and Mary Clare
in *The Hundred Pound
Window*

This comedy, based on a story and screenplay imported from America and Angli-cised, presented Frederick Leister as a clerk promoted to run the Tote's hundred-pound window at a racetrack. He celebrates beyond his means at roulette, but eventually recovers all his losses by accidentally backing a winner. Anne Crawford and Richard Attenborough play his children, while David Farrar is the detective and prospective son-in-law who rounds up a gang of gamblers and black marketeers with the clerk's help.

'Director Hurst has made a bright slick comedy from a strong story . . . in which the numerous twists of plot and incident are never allowed to become tortuous. Freely mixing exteriors and a wide variety of sets, he makes the most of contrast between the home life, the city, the racetrack and "crook" night life. To admirable casting he adds painstaking characterisation which wins from all his actors – a long list – an unusually high standard of work' (*Monthly Film Bulletin*).

Brian Desmond Hurst also directed such films as *Dangerous Moonlight* (1941), *Theirs is the Glory* (1945 documentary), *Scrooge* (1951), *The Malta Story* (1953), and *The Playboy of the Western World* (1962).

1945

Flight from Folly

Pat Kirkwood had played supporting roles in four films some years before. Now a West End musical star, she was given a leading role singing and dancing in *Flight from Folly*. She made a strong impression on the critics ('Pat Kirkwood is in great form', 'an engaging sparkle', 'sparkling performance'), although it did not lead to a film career. She played an out-of-work chorus girl, marking time as a nurse by looking after Hugh Sinclair's playboy composer, who has become neurotic and alcoholic since being jilted by his Russian wife (Tamara Desni). He follows his wife to Majorca, but learns in time to love his nurse instead, and she steps in at the last moment to star in a show featuring his latest songs.

In his last screen role, Sydney Howard had a small but telling part as the playboy's psychiatrist, while A. E. Matthews appeared as a butler.

'This is a frivolous and lively sort of film, elaborately conceived and produced.

Flight from Folly

Director	Herbert Mason
Leading players	Pat Kirkwood
	Hugh Sinclair
	Sydney Howard
	Tamara Desni
	Jean Gillie
	A. E. Matthews
	Marion Spencer
	Leslie Bradley
	Charles Goldner
Screenwriters	Basil Woon,
	Lesley Storm,
	Katherine Strueby
	(from a story by
	Edmund Goulding)
Cinematographer	Otto Heller
Production company/ distributor	Warner Bros
Running time	94 mins

Hugh Sinclair and Pat Kirkwood in *Flight from Folly*

Pat Kirkwood throws herself wholeheartedly into playing the part of Sue, and acts, sings and dances pleasingly' (*Monthly Film Bulletin*).

Even a less complimentary reviewer in the *Daily Mail* concluded that *Flight from Folly* 'does, I think, represent a tremulous but definite step towards a school of British musicals.'

Herbert Mason concluded a nine-year film directing career with *Flight from Folly*, later becoming a producer for Group 3. Earlier films thought lost are *Dr O'Dowd* and *The Night Invader* (both featured in this book) and *Fingers* (1940).

Flight from Folly:
Pat Kirkwood,
A. E. Matthews and
Hugh Sinclair

APPENDICES

The Documentaries

IT IS OFTEN forgotten that cinema began with 'documentary' films. Lumière and Edison shot their first scenes in the garden and in the street, and already by 1900 quite elaborate travelogues and 'interest' films were being made, as well as newsreels and advertising films. Film as a record of the twentieth century is self-evidently of primary importance, and this was recognised by the National Film Archive right at the beginning of its existence in 1935: the preservation of non-fiction film has always been accorded equal status in the NFA alongside the feature and fiction film.

Britain also holds an eminent place in the development of the creative documentary, from the pioneering films of Paul, Williamson and Smith, through the two great periods of the so-called Documentary Movement in the 30s and 40s and Free Cinema in the 60s, to the astonishing range of actuality films made for television today. And like the movie classics, the well-known, written-about documentaries – the *Night Mails*, the *Songs of Ceylon*, the *Nice Times* and the *O Dreamlands* – have largely survived, if not always in the best of shape.

Beyond the mainstream, however, it is difficult to give a precise accounting of all the documentary and non-fiction films which have become lost over the years. By its very non-theatrical nature, this kind of material has, for the most part, been scantily documented and is poorly remembered, if at all – making it virtually impossible to know what it is that is lost. All we do know, from experience, is that every scrap of film which shows an event, a factory at work, a city street, a public figure or a private family outing, especially from the first half of the century, is of potential value to the historian, researcher and film archivist, and should never be discarded without a viewing.

There are, nevertheless, some famous omissions from the preservation vaults which are constantly being sought, of which the following are four significant examples.

On 18 September 1900, Robert W. Paul screened his *Army Life, or How Soldiers are Made* at London's Alhambra Theatre. This was a series of twenty short items intended to illustrate the life and career of a soldier and the work of each branch of the Service. At the time a newspaper review commented: 'It is doubtful whether the Animatograph has ever before been turned to such good account . . . Of exceptional merit combining art and actuality.' Like countless other silent films of the cinema's first decade, this series did not survive, but its loss is clearly of more than passing importance.

A complementary case to *Army Life* is *The New Lot* (1943), one of the most urgently sought-after lost documentaries of the sound era. This, too, was an army training film, written by Peter Ustinov and directed by Carol Reed, which was so successful that it was re-worked the following year to become one of the classic British features of World War II, *The Way Ahead*.

The third example relates to the history of early colour films. Colour was applied to moving images almost from the beginning, to enhance the picture and add drama and realism: hand and stencil colouring and tinting and toning were all used extensively and to various effect. In 1906, G. A. Smith patented a new colour system using filters, which was first demonstrated publicly two years later at the Royal Society of Arts. The system was called Kinemacolor and was widely regarded as the best colour system to date. By 1911, Kinemacolor was being used to cover major news occasions, including the Coronation procession of George V and the Naval Review at Spithead.

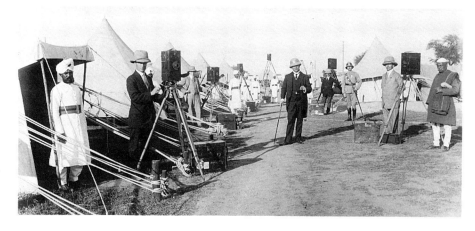

Charles Urban with his Kinemacolor cameramen in Delhi for King George V's Coronation Durbar, 1911

At the end of that year, film impresario Charles Urban and seven of his best cameramen left for India to record in Kinemacolor the Royal Durbar in Delhi. The results of that expedition were shown in London the following February to packed houses. The film lasted an extraordinary six hours. Footage of the Delhi Durbar still exists in black-and-white – but of the great Kinemacolor coverage there is none surviving that we are aware of.

Fourteen years later, Major C. Court Treatt and his wife Stella filmed a journey from *Cape to Cairo* by car via an all-British colonial route, with dumps of spares and food along the way. The Court Treatts went on to film other African material released as *Stampede*. But even though *Cape to Cairo* was released both theatrically and for home distribution on 16 mm, and indeed re-released by Famous Films in 1934, a complete copy of this pioneering travel film is still sought.

There are many examples such as these, known and unknown, and the Archive welcomes any information about the existence of collections, or single copies, of documentaries and non-fiction films, no matter how mundane they may seem. Indeed, it is often the everyday event or activity which encapsulates a time or place more eloquently than the crises of history.

JAMES PATTERSON *Keeper of Documentary Films, National Film Archive*

The Television Programmes

BRITISH TELEVISION has been transmitting programmes for over fifty years, increasing from just a few hours a day on one channel in 1936 to today's round-the-clock coverage on four main channels plus satellite and cable sources. Not all of the enormous current output is preserved, but the mechanisms exist – not least in the National Film Archive – to ensure that anything of significance is likely to survive. However, these mechanisms have only been fully in place since the mid- to late 70s, and the further back in television history you go the fewer programmes or programme items still remain.

Indeed, the earliest material, up to the end of the 50s (which is when the Archive began to acquire television for preservation) can scarcely be described as 'missing' because most of it never existed in a form which could be kept. This is because the vast bulk of programmes were performed and transmitted 'live'. The technology to record them on film was introduced in 1947 but was only sparingly used throughout the 50s, for historic occasions like the Coronation, for some prestige arts and drama performances, for a few selected sporting events, and for a handful of examples of more general programming. Otherwise, most of what remains of British television of the 50s consists of the specially shot film items for topical programmes such as *Tonight* (BBC), *Monitor* (BBC) and *This Week* (Associated Rediffusion). Some programmes, of course, were recorded and then discarded, so it is possible that they still exist, and occasionally lost items do come to light. By and large, though, it is unlikely that there is a great deal of material not in the official national and company archives. Any television programmes from the 50s discovered outside these collections are, therefore, usually valuable finds, and particularly sought-after titles include early *Armchair Theatre* (ABC) productions, especially *No Trams to Lime Street* (1959) by Alun Owen.

With the coming of videotape at the end of the 50s, television programme production switched from being mainly 'live' to being largely pre-recorded. Because of the continued absence of an archival policy, large numbers of programmes were officially discarded, but the fact that so much had been recorded means that some of it may have survived, ironically very often on film recordings transferred from the original videotapes. The National Film Archive and the BBC have had some notable successes in recovering supposedly 'lost' programmes, such as various episodes of *Dr Who* (BBC), *At Last The 1948 Show* (Rediffusion) and *Z-Cars* (BBC). The main sources are foreign television stations, who may have bought a show for transmission and kept the copy; programme production staff, such as the director of Dennis Potter's *A Beast with Two Backs* (BBC, 1968), who kept a cutting copy of the play; and private collectors, whose sources are various but who are often difficult to approach as they fear legal action for a breach of copyright law (needlessly, if they have made no attempt to exploit the material).

It would be almost impossible to produce a complete list of which television programmes are 'missing', so enormous would it be, but there would be particular

A Suitable Case for Treatment: Ian Hendry as Morgan Delt, John Bennett as the policeman, with the firing squad

A for Andromeda: (left to right) Peter Ducrow, Mary Morris, Julie Christie, Peter Halliday, Patricia Kneale

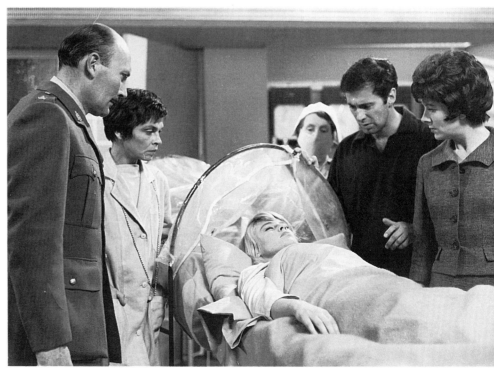

Dandy Nichols and
Warren Mitchell in *Till
Death Us Do Part*

rejoicing over the discovery of such treasures as David Mercer's *A Suitable Case for Treatment* (BBC, 1962), the science fiction series *A for Andromeda* (BBC, 1961), *Sunday Night at the London Palladium* (ATV) or the 60s episodes of *Till Death Us Do Part* (BBC), as well as the titles mentioned above. Material is missing from all genres of television production, including current affairs, sport and the arts, although it is drama and entertainment which always get the most attention.

The rapid obsolescence of video formats gives an added urgency to the search for lost programmes. The National Film Archive has acquired several missing episodes of the classic comedy *Steptoe and Son* from one of the writers, Ray Galton, who kept them on an obsolete half-inch video format. Although they are very difficult to play and provide poor quality reproduction, the significance of this find is such that it provides ample justification for the maintenance of antique machinery and gives added impetus to the continuing search for other lost gems.

STEVE BRYANT *Keeper of Television, National Film Archive*

INDEX

Films

Bed and Breakfast, 31-2
Bella Donna, 53-4
Bells, The, 35-6
Bergadler, Der
    see *Mountain Eagle, The*
Black Mask, 62
Blind Justice, 55
Blue Squadron, The, 51
Born Lucky, 44
Brown Wallet, The, 63-4

C.O.D., 43
Compulsory Wife, The, 78
Condemned to Death, 40
Confidential Lady, 93
Constant Nymph, The, 27

Dangerous Medicine, 88-9
Daredevils of the Earth
    see *Money for Speed*
Dark Stairway, The, 82-3
Dark World, 63
Dr O'Dowd, 92-3
Double or Quits, 87

Educated Evans, 70

Fair Exchange, 68
Faithful, 66-7
Father and Son, 55
Fear o'God
    see *Mountain Eagle, The*
Flight from Folly, 97-8

Gaolbreak, 64-5
Gentleman's Gentleman, A, 91
Get Off My Foot, 61-2
Ghost Train, The, 32-3
Girl in Possession, The, 49-51
Girl in the Crowd, The, 57
Glimpse of Paradise, A, 56
Good Old Days, The, 91-2
Gypsy, 72-3
Gypsy Melody, 69

Hail and Farewell, 71
Hello Sweetheart, 60
Help Yourself, 41
Her Imaginary Lover, 46-7
High Finance, 48
His Brother's Keeper, 94
His Lordship, 43-4

Hundred Pound Window, The, 97

I Adore You, 49
I Married a Spy
    see *Secret Lives*
Irish for Luck, 71-2
It's Not Cricket, 77

Last Hour, The, 31
Lily of the Alley, 23
Lord Babs, 42
Lord Richard in the Pantry, 30
Love, Life and Laughter, 21-2

Man Behind the Mask, The, 65-6
Man Who Made Diamonds, The, 80
Mayfair Melody, 75
Milestones, 21
Mr What's His Name, 59-60
Money for Speed, 45-6
Mountain Eagle, The, 25-6
Murder at Monte Carlo, 57-8
Murder Will Out, 95
My Friend the King, 36

Night Invader, The, 96
No Escape, 52

Office Wife, The, 52-3
On Thin Ice, 45

Price of a Song, The, 58

Quiet, Please, 84

Rasp, The, 37-8
Reveille, 24

Secret Lives, 73-4
She, 19-20
Side Street Angel, 76
Silver Spoon, The, 47
Simply Terrific, 84
Singing Cop, The, 83
Someday, 61
Star Reporter, The, 39-40
Stranglehold, 37
Study in Scarlet, A, 18

Take It From Me
    see *Transatlantic Trouble*
Thank Evans, 86-7

Thistledown, 87-8
Transatlantic Trouble, 79
Twelve Good Men, 67
Two Crowded Hours, 33-4

Ultus 1: The Townsend Mystery
    see *Ultus, the Man from the Dead*
Ultus, the Man from the Dead, 19
Ultus 2: The Ambassador's Diamond
    see *Ultus, the Man from the Dead*

Viper, The, 85
Vulture, The, 74-5

What a Man!, 90
What Next?, 28
What's in a Name?, 56
Where's Sally?, 68
Who Killed John Savage?, 81-2
Windmill, The, 77-8

You Live and Learn, 81

Film-makers

Monty Banks
  Father and Son, 55
  Girl in Possession, The, 49-51
  Hello Sweetheart, 60
Will Barker
  She, 19-20
William Beaudine
  Educated Evans, 70
  Get Off My Foot, 61-2
  Transatlantic Trouble, 79
Thomas Bentley
  Milestones, 21
Adrian Brunel
  Constant Nymph, The, 27

John Y. Daumery
  Help Yourself, 41

Henry Edwards
  Lily of the Alley, 23
  Stranglehold, 37
Maurice Elvey
  Who Killed John Savage?, 81-2

Walter Forde, 12
  Bed and Breakfast, 31-2
  Condemned to Death, 40
  Ghost Train, The, 32-3
  Last Hour, The, 31
  Lord Babs, 42
  Lord Richard in the Pantry, 30
  What Next?, 28

Edmond T. Gréville
  Gypsy Melody, 69
  Secret Lives, 73-4
  What a Man!, 90

Alfred Hitchcock
  Mountain Eagle, The, 25-6
Brian Desmond Hurst
  Hundred Pound Window, The, 97

Ralph Ince, 12-13
  Black Mask, 62
  Fair Exchange, 68
  Gaolbreak, 64-5
  Glimpse of Paradise, A, 56
  Hail and Farewell, 71
  It's Not Cricket, 77
  Man Who Made Diamonds, The, 80
  Mr What's His Name, 59-60

Murder at Monte Carlo, 57-8
No Escape, 52
Side Street Angel, 76
Twelve Good Men, 67
Vulture, The, 74-5
What's in a Name?, 56

George King
  Blue Squadron, The, 51
  Her Imaginary Lover, 46-7
  High Finance, 48
  I Adore You, 49
  Office Wife, The, 52-3
  Silver Spoon, The, 47

Horace Lisle Lucoque
  She, 19-20

Herbert Mason
  Dr O'Dowd, 92-3
  Flight from Folly, 97-8
  Night Invader, The, 96
Max Miller, 13
  Educated Evans, 70
  Get Off My Foot, 61-2
  Thank Evans, 86-7
  Transatlantic Trouble, 79
Robert Milton
  Bella Donna, 53-4

Roy William Neill, 14
  Double or Quits, 87
  Gentleman's Gentleman, A, 91
  Good Old Days, The, 91-2
  Gypsy, 72-3
  His Brother's Keeper, 94
  Murder Will Out, 95
  Quiet, Please, 84
  Simply Terrific, 84
  Thank Evans, 86-7
  Viper, The, 85

George Pearson
  Love, Life and Laughter, 21-2
  Reveille, 24
  Study in Scarlet, A, 18
  Ultus, the Man from the Dead, 19
Michael Powell, 14-15
  Born Lucky, 44
  Brown Wallet, The, 63-4
  C.O.D., 43
  Girl in the Crowd, The, 57

His Lordship, 43-4
Man Behind the Mask, The, 65-6
My Friend the King, 36
Price of a Song, The, 58
Rasp, The, 37-8
Someday, 61
Star Reporter, The, 39-40
Two Crowded Hours, 33-4

Paul L. Stein
  Faithful, 66-7

Harcourt Templeman
  Bells, The, 35-6

Bernard Vorhaus, 15-16
  Blind Justice, 55
  Dark World, 63
  Money for Speed, 45-6
  On Thin Ice, 45

Oscar M. Werndorff
  Bells, The, 35-6
Arthur Woods, 16
  Compulsory Wife, The, 78
  Confidential Lady, 93
  Dangerous Medicine, 88-9
  Dark Stairway, The, 82-3
  Irish for Luck, 71-2
  Mayfair Melody, 75
  Singing Cop, The, 83
  Thistledown, 87-8
  Where's Sally?, 68
  Windmill, The, 77-8
  You Live and Learn, 81